BLESSED ASSURANCE

Blessed Assurance

A History of Evangelicalism in America

RANDALL BALMER

BEACON PRESS

BOSTON

Beacon Press B O S T O N

Beacon Press
25 Beacon Street
Boston, Massachusetts 02108-2892
www.beacon.org

Beacon Press books
are published under the auspices of the Unitarian Universalist
Association of Congregations.

Printed in the United States of America
05 04 03 02 01 00 99   8 7 6 5 4 3 2 1

This book is printed on recycled acid-free paper
that contains at least 20 percent postconsumer waste and meets the uncoated
paper ANSI/NISO specifications for permanence as revised in 1992.

Text design by Lucinda Hitchcock
Composition by Wilsted & Taylor Publishing Services

LIBRARY OF CONGRESS CATALOGING-IN-PUBLICATION DATA

Balmer, Randall Herbert.
Blessed assurance : a history of evangelicalism in America /
Randall Balmer.
p.   cm.
Includes bibliographical references.
ISBN 0-8070-7710-0 (cloth)
1. Evangelicalism—United States—History.   I. Title.
BR1642.U5B34   1999
277.3—dc21   99-24838
CIP

For

Douglas Frank, Mark A. Noll, John Murrin,

and John F. Wilson

MENTORS ALL . . . AND FRIENDS

Contents

A City Upon a Hill

Alexis de Tocqueville may not have said it first, but he probably said it best: "Upon my arrival in the United States," he wrote in 1835, "the religious aspect of the country was the first thing that struck my attention."[1] Others have made similar observations. In 1855, Philip Schaff reported a conversation with a fellow foreigner, who remarked that "the United States [is] by far the most religious and Christian country in the world."[2] Nearly seventy years later, the British writer G. K. Chesterton commented that America thought of itself in religious terms and that the United States was "a nation with the soul of a church."[3]

Any assessment of American history and culture must include an appreciation of the ways in which religion has shaped our national life. You cannot understand nineteenth-century social reform and benevolence societies, for instance, without taking into account the postmillennial optimism growing out of the Second Great Awakening; similarly, any attempt to comprehend nineteenth-century medicine without including the religious ideas of Sylvester Graham, Ellen Gould White, Phineas Parkhurst Quimby, Mary Baker Eddy, or D. D. Palmer would produce an incomplete picture. Taking an even broader perspective, religion and politics within the African-American tradition are so intertwined as to be inseparable, and Americans' dogged resistance to socialism derives, at least in part, from the conviction that good works — medical care, hospitals, and other help for the needy — belong in the *religious* rather than the *political* sphere. American popular culture is steeped in religion. You hear it in the prayers offered before football games and in the lyrics of country music. It crops up on roadside billboards and in the ritual evocations of the Deity in American political discourse.

America's persistent religiosity confounds sociologists and other experts on social evolution who had predicted that as any society modernized and industrialized, religion would be pushed to the periphery – that advances in science and technology would terminate our quaint attachment to religion. But today in the United States, still among the most modern and industrialized of nations, religion both informs public discourse and, for many Americans, lies at the heart of personal identity. Gallup poll data are staggering: 94 percent of Americans believe in God or some supreme being, as compared with 76 percent of the British, 62 percent of the French, and 52 percent of Swedes. More than 90 percent of Americans say they pray at least once a week. In addition, 56 percent claim membership in a church or synagogue, and 40 percent say they attend church, mosque, or synagogue at least once in an average week, compared with 14 percent in Great Britain and 12 percent in France.[4] While those numbers say nothing about the *quality* of religious life in the United States, it is clear that Americans think of themselves as religious.

This persistent religiosity raises several questions. What makes American religion distinctive? How have religion and culture overlapped in America? Why must any responsible examination of American culture include religion?

The United States was the first Western society founded primarily by Protestants rather than Catholics. North America offered a kind of cultural *tabula rasa* for European settlers of many nationalities and religious persuasions, both Protestant and Catholic, who took full advantage of that opportunity. By 1700, the western shores of the Atlantic had become a virtual laboratory of European ethnic and religious diversity, harboring English Puritans in New England; dissenting Baptists in Rhode Island; the Dutch (and countless others) in New York; a polyglot culture in New Jersey that encompassed the Dutch along with Scottish Presbyterians and English Quakers; Moravians, Lutherans, Quakers, and various Anabaptist groups in Pennsylvania; English Catholics in Maryland; and Swedish Lutherans along the Delaware. To the south, Anglicans controlled the religious life of Virginia and Georgia, at least nominally, but they struggled with various folk practices for the religious allegiance of settlers in the backcountry of the Carolinas. Still further south, Spanish Catholics had established a presence in Florida as early as 1528.

The New World gave all of these groups license to begin anew, to leave behind the mistakes, the wounds, and the pretensions of the Old World. It attracted adventurers, those fleeing the institutional constraints of Europe, people not bound by precedent but willing to experiment. Here, it seemed, there was no need to struggle against the ossified traditions of the Old World as embodied in church establishments or universities. The New World, stretching to the west, offered limitless space for experimentation in both social and religious forms, as the nineteenth century would demonstrate. In time, the vast expanses of territory would give rise to regional variations in American religious beliefs and practice, depending upon historical, geographical, and cultural contexts.

Indeed, Americans retain a passion for novelty, and nowhere is it more manifest than in religion. There is a benumbing variety of religious groups in the United States today: Mormons, Methodists, Lutherans, Buddhists, Muslims, Adventists, Swedenborgians, Shakers, Jehovah's Witnesses, Catholics, and countless others – all in numberless variations. Jews in America, for instance, divide themselves into Reform, Conservative, Reconstructionist, and Orthodox camps, and even those labels do not account for the various "families" of Hasidic Jews. There are fifty-some-odd Baptist denominations in America, to say nothing of independent churches and congregations within that tradition.

All of this was made possible by the First Amendment, which in turn had been mandated by the religious pluralism of the eighteenth century. Both too much and too little has been made of the disestablishment of religion in the United States. Scholars and legal theorists have sifted through the tea leaves of history in search of the "original intent" of the founders in providing for what has come to be known as the separation of church and state. In fact, as I argue in the second chapter, the impetus behind the First Amendment lay in an unlikely confederation of rational Enlightenment deists and the New Light Separates of what historians generally refer to as the Great Awakening, the colonies-wide religious revival of the 1730s and 1740s.

Each side sought disestablishment for different reasons. Isaac Backus, a Baptist from Connecticut, sought to protect religion from the state – in Roger Williams's words, to keep the "wilderness of the world" from encroaching upon the "garden of the church" – while Thomas Jefferson and the architects of the Constitution wanted to protect political institutions from religious interference. More than anything else, however, the First Amendment was a political settlement. Jefferson himself was a theorist, an intellectual, an inventor – even a student of the Bible – but above all he was a politician, and the First Amendment was a concession to political realities. American religion in the eighteenth century was already pluralistic, and the founding fathers recognized that they could never impose an established church on all the colonies. There was, moreover, another impediment: Which would be the established religion? Anglicanism, though favored personally by George Washington, was associated with British imperialism. Methodism, organized in America in 1784, was both too new and too closely tied to Anglicanism, having begun as a revival movement within the Church of England. The Quakers of Pennsylvania would almost certainly protest the imposition of any established religion, just as their forebears had done in Flushing, in seventeenth-century New Netherland. The Baptist faith would raise the hackles of New England, and the establishment of Unitarianism would incite insurrections almost everywhere outside of Boston – and perhaps there too. Moreover, every attempt at religious establishment in the individual colonies had been an abject failure. There had been a nominal establishment of Anglicanism in Virginia and Maryland, but similar attempts to establish the Church of England in New York had foundered. Even in New England, the Congregationalist establishment was badly shaken by the Unitarians and the Separate Baptists.

While the First Amendment itself has received a great deal of scrutiny, too little attention has been paid to its *effects* on American life. As I shall argue in this volume, religious disestablishment has helped to ensure political stability in the United States by siphoning social discontent into the religious sphere and away from the political arena. The United States has only two major (centrist) political parties but a wide spectrum of religious beliefs and practices. Religion, then, has tended to protect government from the paroxysms of revolution in part because the First Amendment established a kind of free market of religion.

This *laissez-faire* posture has guaranteed a salubrious religious climate — always innovative and experimental. It has paved the way for religious entrepreneurs, who are always competing for popular followings. For many, the approach is simple: run up a flag, see who salutes — and add them to your mailing list. Charismatic personalities fare best in this climate, and once again the list is endless. The names Joseph Smith, William Miller, Ellen Gould White, Mary Baker Eddy, Noble Drew Ali, Malcolm X, and Jimmy Swaggart come to mind, along with many others. All of them have taken full and proper advantage of the free religious marketplace provided by the First Amendment.

Throughout American history no one has exploited freedom of religion to greater advantage than the itinerant preacher, who emerges as a kind of paradigm of American religious independence, nonconformity, and populism. The itinerancy of the Great Awakening, in the eighteenth century, demolished the aristocratic aspirations and pretensions of the clergy. In their travels throughout the Atlantic colonies, mendicant preachers — with their emphasis on simple, extemporaneous preaching in the vernacular — challenged and even displaced the settled clergy of the eighteenth century and functioned as oracles of the people. The success of these itinerants, as I shall argue, helps to account for one of the most striking characteristics of American religious life: its lack of anticlericalism. Whereas the French Enlightenment was virulently anticlerical, there was relatively little anticlericalism in the Anglo-American Enlightenment. Most of the clergy in the United States have recognized that in the free market of American religious life the secret to their professional longevity has lain not in a reliance upon hierarchy or other traditional levers of religious authority but in catering – even pandering – to the tastes of their various constituencies.

Indeed, some of the most successful religious groups in American history – the Baptists, the Methodists, the Mormons, the Disciples of Christ, to name but a few – have been unabashedly populist. All began as protest movements against what their adherents viewed as elite religious traditions – Puritanism in New England, the Church of England, the various Protestant establishments that claimed a monopoly on biblical truth. All championed the "little person" by insisting that she or he possessed a spirituality superior to that of one elite or another. As Theodorus Jacobus Frelinghuysen, an eighteenth-century Dutch Pietist who preached in New Jersey, put it: "Believers are often poor as to this world. . . . Riches are, frequently, a hindrance in following Jesus; not only because the heart is, usually, too much set upon them, but because they create such reluctance when it is necessary, with Moses, to prefer the reproach of Christ to the treasures of Egypt." [5] Nathan Hatch, a historian of the early Republic, points out that the "single most striking theme in the *Book of Mormon* is that it is the rich, the proud, and the learned who find themselves in the hands of an angry God." [6]

For those concerned with spiritual purity, with the *quality* of religious life in America, such populism comes at a price – a general devaluation of religious commitment and a diminishment of rigor. Especially in the waning decades of the twentieth century, religious groups have become obsessed with membership statistics and Arbitron ratings, both of them indices of popularity. Much of evangelical worship has degenerated into showmanship, with applause and "canned" orchestra music – a naked (and rather successful) quest for popularity in a media culture.

Because of this focus on maintaining large popular followings, evangelicalism in America tends not to demand very much of its adherents for fear of alienating them. At its worst, it tells us we are right, that America is God's chosen land, that we have cornered the market on truth and righteousness, that we know the mind of God. For much of the twentieth century, American religion has effectively "baptized" American consumerism and middle-class values, first with mainline Protestantism's flight to the suburbs in the 1950s and then, more recently, with the widespread propagation of so-called prosperity theology among evangelicals in the 1980s, offering assurance that religion will not only solve the personal problems of believers but also augment their bank accounts. In fact, according to Kenneth Hagin, Frederick Price, and contemporary prosperity propagandists (as for seventeenth-century Puritans), affluence is a sure sign of God's blessing.

Popular religion in America bends with the prevailing winds. Whereas once religion explained the vagaries of the natural world, advances in science have relegated religion more and more to issues of personal well-being. During the last half century, the more popular religious groups have often adapted to this change in circumstance by offering a cornucopia of special-interest and support groups catering to the personal needs of congregants. Religion in this narrowed context becomes a form of therapy and a vehicle for self-improvement.

Because of its relentlessly populist cast, then, religion in America generally offers very little prophetic challenge to American cultural norms and assumptions but instead endorses those norms. To do otherwise would, of course, be unpopular.

This emphasis on populism and popularity in religion, together with a passion for novelty, has led, almost inexorably, to eclecticism. The quest for large popular followings gives rise to a constant shuffling and reshuffling of religious beliefs and opinions in an effort to find a formula that will have widespread appeal. As Jon Butler and David D. Hall have shown, the religious life of colonial America was hardly orthodox. Colonists freely mixed superstitions and occult practices with belief in orthodox Christianity. In 1684, for instance, Harvard College – founded by Puritans who prided themselves on their fidelity to orthodox Christian theology – postponed its commencement because the scheduled date fell too close to that of a solar eclipse.

Later, in the nineteenth century, spiritualists very often exercised their beliefs in the spirit world under the rubric of traditional forms of Protestant worship, repeating the Lord's Prayer, for example, in both their congregational gatherings and at séances. Early Mormonism combined Christianity with conjury and "white magic." And, as William James has written, Christian Science began as an amalgam of the Christian gospels, Berkeleyan idealism, Emersonianism, spiritualism, Hinduism, and positive thinking. More recent examples abound. The Nation of Islam drew upon the Moorish Science Temple, the Jehovah's Witnesses, the life and teachings of Marcus Garvey, and even a smidgen of orthodox Islam. Many of those attracted to the crystals and chakras of the "New Age," all the rage in the 1980s, were reluctant to sacrifice more conventional beliefs; New Age synagogues sprouted, as did "Aquarian rosaries" and the like, and several Roman Catholic theologians, notably David Toolan and Matthew Fox, drew disapproving glares from the Vatican for their advocacy of a "New Age Catholicism."

Equally common among Americans generally has been a personal sort of eclecticism, marked by a breezy willingness to change churches – for example, from Baptist to Methodist to Lutheran – with no sense that (historically, at least) these traditions have very different theologies and confessions. Sheila Larson, a nurse quoted in *Habits of the Heart: Individualism and Commitment in American Life,* published in 1985, expressed the sentiments of countless Americans: "I believe in God. I'm not a religious fanatic. I can't remember the last time I went to church. My faith has carried me a long way. It's Sheilaism. Just my own little voice. . . . It's just to love yourself and be gentle with yourself. You know, I guess, take care of each other. I think He would want us to take care of each other."[7]

Evangelicalism, America's folk religion, courses through American history in erratic and unpredictable ways. According to a 1989 survey, 40 percent of Americans identified themselves as "born again," a designation derived from the Gospel of John that connotes an evangelical conversion experience. America's distinctive forms of evangelicalism emerged from the fusion of New England Puritanism with Continental Pietism, which erupted spectacularly in the Great Awakening, in the middle decades of the eighteenth century. American evangelical theology, in turn, was significantly altered by republicanism later in the same century.

Whereas the Great Awakening of the 1730s and 1740s had been Calvinist, emphasizing the terrors of judgment in reclaiming the elect, the Second Great Awakening, at the turn of the nineteenth century – *after* the American Revolution – was Arminian, that is, it was grounded in an alternative Protestant theology which insists that individuals can initiate the salvation process, that they needn't wait for the call of God. During the Second Great Awakening, revivalist preachers summoned their powers of persuasion in calling sinners to exercise their volition and choose salvation over damnation. In a culture inebriated with self-determinism, and among a people who had only recently taken their *political* destiny into their own hands, this emphasis upon human agency in the salvation process – individuals could *choose* their spiritual destinies rather than relying on the caprices of a distant God – held enormous appeal.

The Second Great Awakening convulsed three theaters of the new nation – New England, western New York, and the Cumberland Valley – and made evangelicalism a formidable force in American history, shaping the social and political agenda for the entire country for much of the nineteenth century. Building upon the fervor of this second religious revival, evangelicals organized and energized many of the social reform and benevolence societies of the nineteenth century, including the temperance, prison reform, abolition, and missionary movements. Evangelicals invested their efforts in such enterprises as female seminaries, Sunday schools, and the mass production and distribution of religious literature: Bibles, tracts, hymnbooks, magazines, journals, and newspapers.

These activities contradict one of the more durable twentieth-century myths about evangelicalism – namely, that evangelicals are somehow suspicious of innovation and modern technology. Nothing could be further from the truth. Evangelicals have embraced technology and innovation throughout their history, especially in the field of communications. As Harry Stout has shown, the open-air preaching of the Great Awakening was appropriated by the Patriots during the American Revolution, who relied on persuasive public rhetoric to galvanize opposition to the Crown. The Methodist genius for organization, especially the use of circuit-riding preachers, provided a model for grassroots political organizations, just as the camp meeting was a precursor of the political rally. In 1826, the American Bible Society installed a steam-powered Treadwell press, the first in New York, and by 1829 the society had sixteen in operation (Harper Brothers publishing company installed its first four years later).[8] In the twentieth century, radio preachers and televangelists used electronic media long before Franklin Roosevelt and Ronald Reagan discovered their value as political tools; and today Pat Robertson's Christian Broadcasting Network in Virginia Beach, Virginia, boasts state-of-the-art television studios and electronics, reputedly the envy of the major networks.

With regard to modernity, then, the issue for evangelicals has never been a skittishness about innovation or technology. Rather, they have been suspicious of assaults on "traditional morality," however variously defined. Much of their discontent centers around the role of women in the household and in society. Adopting the nineteenth-century cult of domesticity, American evangelicals have responded to feminism and the so-called sexual revolution with deep suspicion and have staked out highly conservative and "traditional" positions in politics and family life.

Despite (or perhaps because of) this conservatism, evangelicalism has flourished in the twentieth century, just as it has throughout American history. Consistent with the American ethos, it offers a kind of spiritual upward mobility, a chance to improve your lot in the next world and also (according to the promises of some preachers) in this world as well. More important, evangelicals have mastered the art of oral discourse in a nation of talkers. Evangelicals understand the importance of popular appeal and mass communications, and their style, as I shall argue, has profoundly affected American public discourse.

American religious and political discourse has often identified America with the cause of righteousness. The Puritans believed they were the New Israel, fleeing the Egypt of England for the Promised Land of Massachusetts. American religiosity feeds the sense that America occupies a special place in the divine plan. No less a luminary than Jonathan Edwards believed that the millennium would begin in Northampton, Massachusetts; Joseph Smith, founder of the Church of Jesus Christ of Latter-day Saints, taught that the center stake of Zion would be located in Jackson County, Missouri; and at various times preachers have opined that California was the Garden of Eden.

Indeed, despite historical evidence to the contrary, one of the staples of American religious and political rhetoric is the assertion that the United States was always a Christian nation, that its settlers came not for pecuniary gain but out of a hunger for religious freedom and an altruistic desire to convert the native people to Christianity and bring them the "blessings of civilization." Those nobler impulses did indeed figure into the motives of some settlers, but historical fact does not support such blanket assertions. The myth nevertheless endures, stoked by religious and political rhetoric through the centuries.

This conviction that America occupies a special place in the divine economy can be traced in successive slogans that have articulated America's mission to the world. Eighteenth-century Patriots believed that they were pursuing "the sacred cause of liberty" in prosecuting the War of Independence. In the nineteenth century, the white man's mission to "tame the West" and "civilize the savages" was understood as the "manifest destiny" of the nation. And in the twentieth century, Americans have been engaged in various righteous crusades, from Normandy to Korea, from Iwo Jima to Vietnam, in the name of "making the world safe for democracy."

John Winthrop captured this sentiment, this very American attitude – and its burden – in his sermon aboard the *Arbella*. "Wee shall finde that the God of Israell is among us," he assured his fellow Puritans in 1630, but then he added a dire warning: "Wee must Consider that wee shall be as a Citty upon a Hill, the eies of all people are uppon us."

CHAPTER ONE

Challenging the Routine of Religion
Eighteenth-Century Pietism and the Evangelical Tradition

At its root, the word "evangelical" refers to the Gospels of the New Testament and to the evangelists – Matthew, Mark, Luke, and John, the "messengers of good news" – who wrote them. Martin Luther's "rediscovery of the gospel" in the sixteenth century, however, and the religious reformations it triggered, have added new meanings to the term.

Luther believed that the gospel itself had been lost over the centuries, buried beneath the corruptions of the Roman Catholic church. He also became convinced that the Bible alone – *sola scriptura* – was authoritative in matters of faith and doctrine, thereby challenging the Catholic church's hierarchy and many of its traditions, practices, and sacraments. Furthermore, Luther's reading of the New Testament led him to insist that salvation could not be earned through good works, be they masses, pilgrimages, or acts of charity, but was available only by means of grace. According to Luther, the sacrifice of Christ offered each believer direct access to God, and Luther's notion of "the priesthood of believers" both undermined the authority of the Roman Catholic Church and gave his teachings and those of his followers a democratic cast: We are all equal before God.

Luther's protest against Rome – and the Vatican's belligerent response – unleashed the Protestant Reformation, characterized by the concept of a priesthood of believers, salvation by grace through faith (without the agency of the priesthood or even the sacraments of the church), and a reliance on the Bible alone as the basis of religious authority. The Reformation in turn prompted a hunger for literacy and for vernacular translations of the Bible, so that individuals could read and interpret Scripture for themselves. What Luther could not have anticipated was how eagerly some of his followers would seize this opportunity. Within his own lifetime Luther witnessed – and bemoaned – the splintering of Protestant Christianity into a multitude of groups and sub-groups, all of whom claimed to understand the mind of God through their own particular readings of the Bible.

The general characteristics of the evangelicalism of Luther's day (the Lutheran church in Germany still bears the name *Evangelische*) have carried over to North America, albeit in exaggerated forms. The diffusion of this stream of Protestantism into numberless congregations, denominations, and sects has only increased with the passage of time, as each one of an ever-growing number of evangelical leaders claims to have discovered the *true* meaning of the Bible. Luther's insistence that the individual does not need the mediation of the church, the priesthood, or the sacraments – that the believer enjoys direct access to God through Jesus – has led many evangelicals to be suspicious of ecclesiastical hierarchies and liturgies, and even of the sacraments. Most modern-day evangelicals, for example, depart from Luther on the issue of baptism (Luther wanted to retain the practice of infant baptism, while evangelicals have largely adopted adult or "believer's" baptism), and their theology of the Eucharist, or the Lord's Supper, has tended toward memorialism, that is, the doctrine that the bread and wine of Holy Communion offer little spiritual benefit other than to remind us of the life and death of Jesus.

North American evangelicalism derives from the fusion of two strains of Protestantism, Puritanism and Pietism. These two traditions met on the Atlantic seaboard in the eighteenth century, and their coming together provided the spark that ignited the revivalist fires of the Great Awakening in the 1730s and 1740s.

The movement to "purify" the Church of England of all vestiges of Roman Catholicism arose in the late 1500s as part of the Protestant Reformation. When it became clear, late in the 1620s, that they would not succeed to their satisfaction, a group of English Puritans led by John Winthrop secured a charter for the colonization of Massachusetts Bay and set sail for the New World, arriving in 1630 for the purpose of establishing a "city on a hill," a beacon of godliness to the rest of the world, and specifically to England.

Over the ensuing decades these New England Puritans sought to carve a godly commonwealth out of the "howling wilderness" of Massachusetts. By the latter half of the seventeenth century, however, what the Puritan clergy described as "declension" had set in. The community had fallen short of the standards of godliness set by the first generation. The rise of the merchant class had undermined the original Puritan vision, and there was evidence aplenty of God's displeasure: drought, fires in Boston, and King Philip's War (against the native inhabitants of the country, the bloodiest war per capita in American history). In short, the Puritans' bold experiment had failed, and by the early decades of the eighteenth century the ministers were calling the people of New England to repentance.

If the story of Puritanism is fairly well known, that of Pietism, the second partner in the encounter that produced evangelicalism in America, remains rather more obscure. Indeed, there are obstacles aplenty to appreciating Pietism and the role it has played in shaping American religious history.

First, there is the question of definition. The *Oxford English Dictionary* defines Pietism as a movement begun by Philipp Jakob Spener at Frankfurt am Main, Germany, "for the revival and advancement of piety in the Lutheran church" and characterized by a "devotion to religious feeling, or to strictness of religious practice."[1] Such a definition rightly points out the interiority or inner-directedness of Pietist faith, but it ignores the earlier development of Reformed Pietism (or "precisianism") in the Netherlands.[2] It also slights the institutional dimensions of Pietism and fails to capture the ecumenical nature of the movement, which in turn compounds the difficulties of definition because Pietism transcended confessional boundaries and took different forms within different traditions.

Indeed, Pietism spread across the whole Protestant spectrum, from conservative, orthodox, liturgical state-church traditions to separatist groups who reviled the "four dumb idols" of the state churches (the baptismal font, the altar, the pulpit, and, in Lutheran lands, the confessional) to radical prophetic groups alienated from both social and institutional church life. What Pietists of all persuasions held in common was an emphasis on spiritual discipline and affective religion rather than intellectual assent, and a bias against ecclesiastical hierarchies and religious pretensions. Pietism, moreover, can also be viewed in the context of a larger revival of religious fervor and revolt against formality, ceremonialism, scholasticism, and moral laxity; when defined broadly, this larger context encompasses quietism among Roman Catholics in France, Spain, and Italy, Wesleyanism in England, and even Hasidism in eastern Europe.

A second obstacle facing the student of Pietism in the colonies is the scantiness of the literary record, at least relative to the amount of material that has come down to us from the Puritans of New England. In some instances the records are adequate, as in the case of Heinrich Melchior Mühlenberg's *Journals* or the sermons of Theodorus Jacobus Frelinghuysen.[3] And some of the surviving literature, from Johann Conrad Beissel's mystical writings to Bernardus Freeman's "Mirror of Self-Knowledge," displays familiar Pietistic themes: a call for experiential or "experimental" religion, strongly sexual imagery, and an emphasis on mystical introspection, known in the argot of eighteenth-century Pietism as self-knowledge.[4] However, such important Pietists as Peter Henry Dorsius and Guiliam Bertholf, who preached in the Middle Colonies, bequeathed little or nothing to historians, and the whole of John Henry Goetschius's sole published sermon has only recently been made available in English translation.[5] Accounts of contemporaries offer tantalizing glimpses of the lives and careers of Lars Tollstadius and Johann Bernhard van Dieren, but we have nothing from their own pens to help us assess their work and influence more precisely.[6]

The third obstacle is the consequence of a general neglect, on the part of historians, of the Middle Colonies and the rich fabric of ethnic diversity therein. We are just now beginning to understand the variegated texture of ethnic life in the mid-Atlantic colonies –

the lives and influence of the Scots, the Dutch, the Huguenots, the Swedes, the Germans. It is becoming more and more apparent that religion played an important role in shaping the responses of these various ethnic groups to an eighteenth-century colonial culture increasingly defined by the English.[7]

Having catalogued the difficulties in coming to terms with this subterranean world of eighteenth-century Pietism in America, what are the benefits of perseverance? Most important, an appreciation of Pietism has several implications for our understanding of the eighteenth-century revival of religion known as the Great Awakening, which, at least in the Middle Colonies, looks more like an eruption of longer-term Pietistic impulses than the last gasp of Puritanism, and which is directly relevant to evangelicalism in the United States today.

Even a cursory examination of the extant Pietist literature, much of it published in the decades just before the Awakening, reveals some recurrent themes generally associated with that revival – the necessity of spiritual rebirth, for instance, and insistent calls for probity. The Pietist view of the world, moreover, had been sustained in America since the late seventeenth century by irregular preaching and (mostly unaccompanied) hymn-singing, which directed Pietist expressions of faith into informal, nontraditional channels and thus helped to propel the whole revival movement toward the acceptance of itinerant preachers and lay leadership. At the same time that Congregationalist minister Solomon Stoddard reported "harvests" in the Connecticut Valley, Guiliam Bertholf enjoyed considerable success in organizing Pietistic congregations in northern New Jersey, and the Pietistic preaching of Lars Tollstadius created schisms among Swedish Lutherans in the Delaware Valley.

Indeed, a whole range of Pietists tapped into popular discontent among the rural peoples of the Middle Colonies. The list includes Bertholf, Tollstadius, Dorsius, Freeman, Mühlenberg, and Frelinghuysen, but also such lesser-known figures as Cornelius Van Santvoord and Samuel Verbryck (among many others). Even Gilbert Tennent, who was schooled in Pietism at the feet of Frelinghuysen when the two men were colleagues in the Raritan Valley, must be included in this camp: witness his evangelical vigor, his emphasis on a warm-hearted piety, and his assault on the settled clergy in *The Danger of an Unconverted Ministry*.[8]

Tennent's connection with Frelinghuysen underscores another characteristic of Pietism, namely its ecumenical, transatlantic character. The works of such English Puritans as William Perkins and William Ames had been translated into Dutch; Perkins, in turn, had been influenced by the ideas of Willem Teelinck, Godefridus Cornelisz Udemans, and Gysbertus Voetius.[9] In New Jersey, Tennent openly acknowledged his debt to Frelinghuysen, and the two men regularly traded pulpits and often officiated jointly at services. Both George Whitefield and Jonathan Edwards praised Frelinghuysen's efforts in New Jersey. Mühlenberg frequently preached in Dutch churches, and Frelinghuysen's partisans supported Lutheran evangelicals in the Middle Colonies. By the 1750s, the distinction between the Pietistic Dutch and New Light Presbyterians was so slight that William Livingston, publisher of the *Independent Reflector*, remarked that "the different languages are the only criteria to distinguish them from each other."[10] Even that barrier eroded as the Great Awakening pushed Dutch Pietists into the mainstream of eighteenth-century evangelicalism. Henceforth the line between Pietism and evangelicalism in American religion becomes increasingly blurred.

Pietism was very much a transatlantic movement. Unlike the Puritans, whose settlement in New England represented a break with Old World institutions (despite their protestations about remaining members of the Church of England), colonial Pietists maintained close ties with their confrères on the Continent well into the eighteenth century. The Dutch Labadists, for instance, followers of a radical separatist named Jean de Labadie, sought to establish a colony in the New World, and many among the colonial Dutch admired Jacobus Koelman, a sometime disciple of Labadie back in the Netherlands. When Frelinghuysen, who acknowledged his theological indebtedness to

Koelman, sailed across the Atlantic toward his assignment in Raritan, New Jersey, he boasted that after he had worked "to secure a following" in America "immediately many more would come from Holland to his support" – and indeed they did. [11] The German region of Halle, another center of Pietism, supplied pastors to Pennsylvania under the loose supervision of Heinrich Mühlenberg, while immigrants from Württemberg formed the congregations. The Moravians maintained a presence in both Europe and the American colonies.

American Pietism, then, was not an indigenous movement. It had deep roots in the Old World – especially in Holland and Germany – and continued to draw its inspiration from those sources until New World Pietists were able to develop indigenous leadership through individual tutorials, small "kitchen seminaries" like that of Peter Henry Dorsius in Bucks County, Pennsylvania, and, eventually, institutions such as the Dutch Reformed Coetus (1747) and Queen's College (1766) in New Brunswick, New Jersey.

This is not to say, however, that Pietism on the western shores of the Atlantic was identical to that back on the Continent. Keeping "orthodox" doctrinal churches and Pietist renewal groups together was difficult enough in the European context, but once immigrants of diverse backgrounds arrived in America, the spectrum of Pietism tilted sharply toward a more radical version of the movement – witness, for example, Johann Conrad Beissel's Ephrata Community in Pennsylvania, which combined Pietistic impulses with a sort of Catholic mysticism and monasticism, and Samuel Verbryck's insistence on dispensing with the traditional forms of prayer for Easter Sunday and instead preaching a sermon on the crucifixion, in order to demonstrate his disregard for ecclesiastical holidays. [12] Some Pietists, like Mühlenberg among the Lutherans, continued to insist on a balance between orthodox doctrine and Pietist renewal. More often than not, however, what would have been regarded as somewhat daring in a European context was more or less unexceptional in the American setting, where radicalism of a sort tolerated almost nowhere in Europe took root and flourished.

On both continents, eighteenth-century Pietism's most profound effects were certainly on the inner lives of believers who found religious renewal and assurance amid the ferment of revival. As historians, we can point to certain figures – Gilbert Tennent, for instance, or John Wesley – whose lives and ministries were profoundly influenced by Pietistic ideals, and we can identify congregations in the throes of revival, but we shall never know the full meaning of Pietism in the lives of individual "ordinary" colonists.

We do know, however, that Pietism profoundly influenced the *institutional* life of eighteenth-century America, although some of its effects were oddly divergent because Pietism, by its nature a very elastic movement, took on various characteristics within different traditions. Among the Dutch and the New Light Presbyterians, Pietistic impulses reshaped colonial ecclesiastical structures and created an almost iconoclastic movement. It generally did not, however, serve the same radical function among the Germans, Reformed or Lutheran.

There are a few scattered references to the disruptions of Pietism within German communities. (In 1709, for instance, the Governor's Council in New York learned that nineteen of the forty-seven Palatines along the Hudson River had "changed their religion become Pietists and withdrawn themselves from the Communion of the Minister and ye Rest of ye said Germans.")[13] On the whole, however, Pietism among the German immigrants was a source of unity, not division, and when the colonial Lutherans finally organized their ministerium (or synod) in 1748, that body was controlled by Halle Pietists.[14] For the Lutherans, the influence of Mühlenberg and the Halle connection may have been crucial. This influence domesticated Pietism and made it both a means for organizing congregations and a vibrant source of deep personal and communal piety. At the same time, Lutheranism was respectable, and it was sustained by the transatlantic charities and pastoral supply at Halle, which was disbursed through London. Those connections were hardly conducive to radical protest against prevailing norms.

Among the German Reformed ministers, Pietist tendencies seem never to have been very pronounced, with the exception, perhaps, of Peter Henry Dorsius. German Reformed communities were sustained by support from the Swiss and the Dutch; they never enjoyed the substantial monetary resources or the clerical density that their fellow Germans possessed. Moreover, there were many free church and sectarian groups to their left, and German Pietists, whether Reformed or Lutheran, had little inclination or reason to be associated with them. Moravians in particular, thoroughly steeped in more emotional forms of Pietism, were regarded with disdain, especially by the Lutherans, and these feelings were reciprocated. Nevertheless, the Germans had an entire spectrum of ethnic religious options – the Amish, Mennonites, Schwenckfelders, Moravians, Lutherans, Reformed – available to them to accommodate theological and ecclesiastical differences.

Dutch Pietists in the colonies, locked within the confining orbit of the orthodox Dutch Reformed Church, had fewer choices. Either they would join forces with the Presbyterians (as many threatened to do) or they would recast the Dutch Reformed Church in their own image. As their numbers and influence increased, the latter option grew more and more attractive.

Among the Dutch, then, Pietism functioned largely as a theology of the people, a protest against the clerical establishment. Although Pietism certainly had its own positive agenda – revitalization of liturgy and worship, closer attention to personal probity – it also represented a challenge to the ecclesiastical hierarchy. Pietists first organized themselves into conventicles, which, like John Wesley's "methodist" gatherings, sought the infusion of spiritual ardor into religious traditions that had grown stuffy and cold. In the Netherlands, Dutch Pietists had challenged the corruptions of wealth attending the growth of Holland's commercial empire and the arid scholasticism into which seventeenth-century Reformed theologians had fallen. Indeed, Pietism among the Dutch, both in the Netherlands and in the New World, represented a rural protest against the urban elite and the urban clergy as well as a general protest against the ecclesiastical hierarchy of the Dutch Reformed Church as a whole.[15] The Classes (ruling ecclesiastical bodies) of Middleburg, Schieland, and Lingen, for instance, were Pietistic, whereas the Classis of Amsterdam sought to stanch the spread of Pietism on both sides of the Atlantic. The universities of Utrecht and Groningen turned out Pietists, who then very often clashed with graduates of the University of Leiden.

Frustrated in their attempts to dislodge the traditionalist clergy who opposed the Pietist renewal, Dutch Pietists unleashed an attack against the ecclesiastical hierarchy in New York and especially against the Classis of Amsterdam, which sought to thwart the spread of Pietism in the New World. Indeed, Dutch Pietists regarded Amsterdam as the mortal enemy of true religion. Guiliam Bertholf, a cooper from New Jersey and a lay reader for some of the fledgling Dutch congregations on the frontier, knew that the Classis of Amsterdam would never approve his ordination because of his Pietistic leanings and his lack of formal education, so he circumvented Amsterdam completely and was ordained by the Classis of Middleburg. Upon his return to New Jersey in 1694, Bertholf worked tirelessly to organize Pietistic congregations on the New Jersey frontier.[16]

Bernardus Freeman, another Pietist, also nursed a grudge against the Classis of Amsterdam. When the Dutch church at Albany needed a new minister in 1699, Freeman, a tailor by trade, submitted his name. The Classis, however, denied his application and belittled him as someone "who had only just come down from his cutting board, and who had neither ability for his own craft, much less for that demanded of a pastor."[17] With the help of Willem Bancker, an Amsterdam merchant and patron to Pietists in the Netherlands, Freeman sought and received ordination from the Classis of Lingen and sailed for the New World to claim the pastorate at Albany. Amsterdam's candidate, Johannes Lydius, prevailed in that initial ecclesiastical skirmish, but Freeman took the church in nearby Schenectady; several years later, through a series of perfidious maneuvers, he insinuated himself into the Dutch churches on Long Island. Freeman steadfastly refused to submit to the Classis of Amsterdam, and he summarily dismissed those consistories (church councils) that opposed him. His obstinacy precipitated a bitter schism that lasted the better part of a decade and markedly diminished the Classis of Amsterdam's grip on the colony's churches. [18]

Although Theodorus Jacobus Frelinghuysen came to the New World with Amsterdam's formal approbation, after his arrival he made no secret of his intention to flout his independence from the Amsterdam ecclesiastical authorities. Within days of disembarking in New York, Frelinghuysen insulted — and alienated — the traditionalist clergy in New York, declared his disdain for the Classis of Amsterdam, and announced his intention to flood the Middle Colonies with Pietistic clergy. His clerical career in New Jersey was marked by bitter disputes between his evangelical followers and his generally more prosperous detractors in both New Jersey and New York. Because of Amsterdam's suspicions about Pietism, moreover, Frelinghuysen's agenda for the New World implied a circumvention of Amsterdam's ecclesiastical prerogatives. He eagerly took that step. Frelinghuysen, moreover, together with Bertholf and Freeman, supported the incursion of other Pietists in the Middle Colonies, once again over Amsterdam's objections.

Dutch Pietists in general and Frelinghuysen in particular used the language of piety to assail the ecclesiastical establishment and their theological opponents. Frelinghuysen regularly taunted his adversaries. He restricted access to Holy Communion in his Raritan churches, excommunicated dissenters, and angered the more affluent of his auditors when he suggested that "it has been very true that the largest portion of the faithful have been poor and of little account in the world." [19] Despite debilitating bouts of mental illness and unrefuted allegations of homosexuality against him, Frelinghuysen persisted in his attacks on the Classis of Amsterdam and the non-Pietist Dutch ministers. When disaffected members of his congregations drafted a bill of particulars against him and took their case to the New York clergy, Frelinghuysen and his consistory became defiant, resolving unanimously that they would "never suffer any church or pastor in the land to assume dominion over us." [20]

When his mental incapacities finally disabled him, Frelinghuysen's struggle against the ecclesiastical establishment was taken up by an entire cohort of younger men, including his sons and John Henry Goetschius, who became minister on Long Island over the strenuous objections of the Dutch Reformed establishment. Once installed there, Goetschius vigorously assailed his ecclesiastical adversaries. On August 22, 1742, he preached a sermon entitled "The Unknown God," in the course of which he reviled the mere practice of religion, which he contrasted with true spirituality, and he warned his adversaries, "You will experience your religion in hell, and not in heaven, as you had hoped." When called before the New York ministers to account for his attacks, Goetschius remarked that his opponents were "plainly godless people" and that were it not for the Netherlands church authorities, "this country had long ago been filled with pious ministers."[21]

As the number of Pietist clergy increased, these desultory attacks on the ecclesiastical establishment evolved into an orchestrated assault on the Classis of Amsterdam in the Netherlands and the traditionalist clergy in New York. Freeman, Frelinghuysen, Goetschius, and other Dutch ministers openly defied the Classis of Amsterdam on matters of ordination, church polity, and ecclesiastical discipline. In the 1740s, amid the fervor of the Great Awakening, they began agitating for an independent, indigenous ecclesiastical body, a *coetus*, that would govern the American churches. When gaveled to order on September 8, 1747, the Coetus consisted almost entirely of Pietist clergy, all of whom were eager to distance themselves from the Classis of Amsterdam. Within a very few years, members of the Coetus circulated proposals for the formation of both an American classis and an American academy for the training of Pietistic clergy, and after the American Revolution they would declare their formal independence from the Netherlands church authorities.[22]

This protest against the religious establishment among the Dutch had taken on specifically political overtones, as contemporaries recognized. After the colonial Pietists had banded together to form their Coetus in 1747, one anti-Pietist predicted that if "we should complain about anything to the Classis or the Synod, that our Dutch churches were not regulated after the manner of the churches of the Fatherland, it would be said, 'Oh, the people of Holland govern *their* churches in *their* own way, and we find no fault with them; and we govern our churches, and we are no longer under obligations to give account of our doing to them.'" Others detected "a spirit of independence . . . clearly manifest" in the Pietists' machinations. In the 1750s, when Theodore Frelinghuysen of Albany (a son of Theodorus Jacobus) proposed the establishment of a Pietist American seminary independent of the Netherlands authorities, his conservative opponents asked if his next step was to "rebel against the king."[23]

Indeed, not long after the Dutch Pietist clergy in the Middle Colonies asserted their ecclesiastical independence from the Classis of Amsterdam by forming the Coetus, many of these same ministers — notably Theodore Frelinghuysen, Archibald Laidlie, Johannes Leydt, Dirck Romeyn, and Eilardus Westerlo — joined the chorus calling for political independence for the colonies as well. During the throes of the Stamp Act crisis, for instance, Laidlie preached what at least one auditor considered a "sed[i]t[iou]s sermon" for the purpose of "exciting people to Reb[e]ll[io]n."[24]

The rhetoric about ecclesiastical "liberty" and the aversion to "subordination" that saturated the Dutch Pietists' communications with the Netherlands very easily transferred to the political sphere.[25] Discussions about ecclesiastical liberty and suspicions about the motives of wealthy and learned people, lay and clerical, erupted even among conservative German congregations in the late 1750s and early 1760s, just as the imperial crisis was breaking. For these congregations, steeped in a different Pietist tradition but likewise suspicious of church authorities and controlled by the laity, the language of piety, with its anti-authoritarian overtones, served as a model for thinking in political terms — a first among a largely apolitical people.[26]

Pietism in the Middle Colonies, then, as articulated by those alienated in some way from the religious establishment, provided a radical critique of eighteenth-century authority structures, first religious and then political. The exercise of lay initiative and a suspicion of clerical prerogative were deeply imbedded in the Pietist tradition, and, for Dutch Pietists at least, the assertion of ecclesiastical independence led quite logically, almost seamlessly, to the assertion of political independence. Pietism, then, the earliest harbinger of the religious revival of the 1730s and 1740s, provides a new key for understanding both ecclesiastical and political activism in the Middle Colonies during the eighteenth century.

After the middle of the eighteenth century, Continental Pietism as an identifiable movement within the colonies largely disappeared into the mainstream of American religious life, much in the way that the Mohawk River flows into the Hudson or the Schuylkill into the Delaware. Theodorus Jacobus Frelinghuysen's machinations in the Raritan Valley had produced both revival and reaction in the 1720s, and his friendship with Gilbert Tennent introduced the Presbyterian minister to Pietistic traditions, disciplines, and techniques. Tennent then carried the message throughout the Middle Colonies and to New England during his several missionary sorties there. The influences were reciprocal. Pietist congregations in the Middle Colonies welcomed Tennent and George Whitefield, and when Theodorus Frelinghuysen's son Theodore preached a sermon to New England troops during the French and Indian War, it sounded for all the world like a Puritan jeremiad, full of lamentations and apocalyptic warnings.

The ferment of the Great Awakening, together with a number of circumstances and cultural changes thereafter, conspired to obfuscate the influence of Continental Pietism on American religion. For the colonists of Dutch origin, internal conflicts, the desire to enjoy the commercial advantages of assimilation, and a gradual neglect of the Dutch language in favor of English combined to drive their communities away from their hereditary culture toward either Anglicanism or Presbyterianism. Later, and on a larger scale, the importation and rapid success of Methodism in America largely coopted Pietistic expressions of faith (with the exception, once again, of the Germans). John Wesley himself had been influenced by such Continental Pietists as Johann Albrecht Bengel, and he greatly admired the Moravians for their "faith and love and holy conversation in Christ Jesus."[27] Methodist itinerants in America, moreover, had come into contact with Pietist preachers. By the first decades of the new Republic, then, the protest against deficient personal morality, intransigent ecclesiastical establishments, and worldly elites had been taken up by the Methodists and other populist evangelical groups.[28]

What then is the legacy of eighteenth-century Pietism to American religion? Some Pietists of German descent continue, against great odds, to retain their ethnic particularity, their cultural insularity, and their rootedness in Old World traditions. This is surely Pietism's most visible manifestation in America today. Evangelical fervor has also benefited from time to time from the continued infusion of Pietistic groups from the Old World – witness, for example, the immigration of Dutch Seceders in the nineteenth century (who formed the Christian Reformed Church), of the Janssonists from Sweden who settled Bishop Hill, Illinois, and of the Scandinavians of the late nineteenth century who eventually formed the Evangelical Covenant Church and the Evangelical Free Church denominations.[29]

And Pietism – although unlabeled and unrecognized as such – has insinuated itself into the pastische of American religion, especially evangelicalism, in other, less tangible ways. The evangelical prayer meeting of today looks quite a lot like the Pietist conventicles and "methodist" gatherings of the eighteenth century, and all three resemble the nineteenth-century prayer and Bible study session conducted in a Scandinavian *Bede Hus* (prayer house).

The most profound influence of Pietism is, once again, incalculable – its effect upon ordinary believers. For anyone reared within the evangelical subculture in America, with its parietal rules, its emphasis on personal piety, its proscriptions against alcohol, tobacco, and dancing, and its sabbatarian scruples, the continued influence of Pietism is self-evident. Countless evangelists have summoned their auditors to exacting **standard**s of personal probity and spiritual piety, even when they themselves (like Frelinghuysen the elder) fell shy of meeting those standards. An emphasis upon self-examination as prelude to conversion or rededication is the common thread, and in the hands of such acknowledged masters as Charles Grandison Finney, Dwight Lyman Moody, Aimee Semple McPherson, Billy Graham, and even Jimmy Swaggart, it has continued to serve as a powerful tool for revival.

The literature of colonial Pietism also bears many similarities to that of American evangelicalism. Both Pietistic and evangelical sermons are replete with graphic descriptions of the torments of hell and the perils of unbelief or, more subtly, the consequences of a false sense of security among those who merely practice religion in its outward forms and never know the experience of conversion. When Theodorus Jacobus Frelinghuysen implored, "O Sinner! abandon your Way which seemeth so right unto you, your careless and secure Tranquility, your own Righteousness, your Sins and Lusts, your own Thoughts and turn to the Lord," he might have been writing a script for Finney, Moody, Graham, Swaggart, or any one of a thousand other evangelists.[30] The devotional literature of both nineteenth- and twentieth-century evangelicalism also echoes the introspective mode of eighteenth-century Pietistic treatises. The potent sexual imagery of Beissel and Frelinghuysen reverberates in such staples of the evangelical hymnal as "Blessed Assurance," "Jesus, Lover of My Soul," "Just as I Am," and "Rock of Ages, Cleft for Me."

In America, moreover, evangelicals continue to use the argot of piety as a protest against ecclesiastical establishments. The fundamentalist-modernist controversy of the 1920s comes to mind, as does Carl McIntire's rhetoric directed against the "godless" Federal Council of Churches. American fundamentalists, frustrated in their attempts to reverse the drift toward cultural modernism within mainline denominations and their institutions, abandoned them and built their own denominations, Bible institutes, colleges, and seminaries. These actions would not be at all alien to the eighteenth-century progenitors of New Side Presbyterianism, the Dutch Coetus, Queen's College, or the College of New Jersey, nor would it surprise the leaders of the Cumberland Presbyterians or the holiness movement. Throughout its history, evangelicalism, with its roots in Pietism, has mounted strident – and quite effective – attacks on recalcitrant and unresponsive ecclesiastical bureaucracies.

Very often those attacks have been personal, directed against "unconverted" or "liberal" clergy. In that way, the rhetoric of Carl McIntire or Billy Sunday or J. Gresham Machen recalls Gilbert Tennent's *Danger of an Unconverted Ministry*, Frelinghuysen's relentless verbal assaults on his clerical adversaries (as when he criticized them as "unprofitable sickmaking Physicians"), and John Henry Goetschius's sermon "The Unknown God," which lambasted the opponents of true piety as those who impose "their old, rotten, and stinking routine of religion."[31]

Adherents of Pietism in America, in its various guises from the eighteenth century to the present, have assiduously sought to avoid the "routine of religion," preferring instead a vibrant, experiential spiritual life. This in turn has meant that almost by definition, Pietistic impulses transcend institutional, confessional, and ethnic boundaries. Just as Theodorus Jacobus Frelinghuysen and Gilbert Tennent crossed ecclesiastical boundaries in the eighteenth century (much to the scandal of their antirevivalist contemporaries), so too evangelicals have managed at various points in their history to submerge their differences. The ecumenism of the Second Great Awakening comes to mind, as does the Evangelical United Front, the urban revivals of 1858, and the interfaith cooperation that attends Billy Graham's "crusades."

Continental Pietism, New England Puritanism, and the Great Awakening testify to a thirst for authentic religious experience, a challenge to the routine of religion. Much of what these movements shared has persisted in American evangelicalism: exacting standards of morality; a suspicion of liturgical formalism, theological scholasticism, and ecclesiastical structures; an insistent call for conversion juxtaposed with warnings about the torments of hell; and a willingness to cross ethnic and ecclesiatical boundaries. Both Puritanism and Pietism insisted on a warmhearted piety as the basis for salvation and the sign of regeneration. Without "true and experienced knowledge God is still unknown and all religion is idle," John Henry Goetschius preached in 1742.[32]

Billy Graham could not have said it better.

CHAPTER TWO

Diversity and Stability

The Paradox of Religious Pluralism

"*Congress shall make no law* respecting an establishment of religion, or prohibiting the free exercise thereof," the First Amendment to the United States Constitution states straightforwardly, and this simple principle, unprecedented in Western societies, has always attracted a good deal of notice from historians and legal scholars. "Religion in America takes no direct part in the government of society," Alexis de Tocqueville observed, "but nevertheless it must be regarded as the foremost of the political institutions of that country; for if it does not impart a taste for freedom, it facilitates the use of free institutions." [1] De Tocqueville was not the last to remark upon the unique relation of church and state, religion and politics, in American society.

In 1844, historian Robert Baird extolled the voluntary principle in the United States as the "great alternative" to all European societies and their long, troubled history of church-state entanglements. "Religious liberty, fettered by no State enactment," Baird wrote, "is as perfect as it can be." [2] Although Philip Schaff, a native of Germany, harbored some old-fashioned notions about the unity of the church and the ability of Christianity to "leaven and sanctify all spheres of human life," in 1855 he offered grudging admiration for the American configuration of church and state, which he regarded as a "peculiarity in the ecclesiastical condition of North America." [3]

The willingness to give free rein to religious expression, to eschew an establishment, and to countenance the ambiguity arising from that social and political configuration has prompted twentieth-century historian Sidney E. Mead to characterize the relation of church and state in the United States as a "lively experiment."[4] His contemporary Winthrop Hudson defined voluntarism in America and the equilibrium between church and state as the "great tradition of the American churches."[5]

Historians have argued that although it was indeed unprecedented, the impetus for religious disestablishment as embodied in the First Amendment grew out of disparate impulses dating back at least to the Protestant Reformation. Martin Luther's emphasis on the priesthood of believers and each individual's responsibility before God led almost inevitably (if not immediately) to the concession that people might approach God differently, and the splintering of Christianity after the Reformation demanded some sort of accommodation on the part of government and society to religious diversity. Several of the American colonies had done just that; Thomas Jefferson cited the examples of New York and Pennsylvania, which tolerated many denominations, in his *Notes on the State of Virginia*, written in 1781. In other colonies, however, such groups as the Anglicans in Maryland and Virginia, and the Congregationalists in Massachusetts and Connecticut, stubbornly defended their establishment status. Several historians look to such figures and movements as Isaac Backus and the Separate Baptists in Connecticut or William Livingston and the Presbyterian party in New York as influential opponents of religious establishment.[6] Most often, however, when historians retrace the steps of religious disestablishment in America their paths lead to Roger Williams, in the seventeenth century, and to Jefferson himself.

Williams, a Puritan minister at Salem, Massachusetts, had grown increasingly uneasy about the continued identification of New England Puritanism with the Church of England. In 1635, the General Court of Massachusetts brought charges against him for disrupting the social and religious order of New England by proposing that the church at Salem separate completely from the other Massachusetts churches. The General Court banished Williams from the colony, whereupon he fled south, in January 1636, and founded Providence, which eventually became the charter colony of Rhode Island.

In 1644, responding to a letter from John Cotton, a prominent Puritan divine, Williams set out his views regarding the relation of church and state. "When they have opened a gap in the hedge or wall of separation between the garden of the church and the wilderness of the world," he wrote, "God hath ever broke down the wall itself, removed the candlestick, and made His garden a wilderness, as at this day."[7] Williams sought to protect religion from the depredations of the state, and he saw strict separation as the way to accomplish this. If God, Williams believed, "will ever please to restore His garden and paradise again, it must of necessity be walled in peculiarly unto Himself from the world; and that all that shall be saved out of the world are to be transplanted out of the wilderness of the world, and added unto His church or garden."[8]

A little over a hundred years later, Thomas Jefferson appropriated the "wall of separation" metaphor but toward somewhat different ends. Jefferson, a deist and a creature of the Enlightenment, believed passionately that religious beliefs were a private affair, that religious coercion violated natural rights, and that compelling someone "to furnish contributions of money for the propagation of opinions which he disbelieves and abhors" constituted a form of tyranny.[9] Religious disestablishment, Jefferson believed, provided guarantees against such tyranny. Writing nearly two decades after the ratification of the First Amendment (he had been among its principal architects), Jefferson attested to his "solemn reverence for that act of the whole American people which declared that their legislature should 'make no law respecting an establishment of religion, or prohibiting the free exercise thereof,' thus building a wall of separation between church and State."[10]

Although Jefferson had carefully couched his rhetoric so as to appear that he wished merely to provide for the well-being of organized religion by guarding it against political meddling, it is difficult to escape the impression that he was at least equally concerned that religious factionalism and contentiousness might disrupt the functions of government. While serving as president, he considered the "experiment" in religious freedom that he had helped to create in the new

Republic and pronounced it good precisely because it had proved conducive to political order and stability. "We have solved by fair experiment, the great and interesting question whether freedom is compatible with order in government, and obedience to the laws," he wrote to a group of Virginia Baptists in 1802. "And we have experienced the quiet as well as the comfort which results from leaving everyone to profess freely and openly those principles of religion which are the inductions of his own reason, and the serious convictions of his own inquiries."[11]

Both Roger Williams and Thomas Jefferson, then, although separated by more than a century, advocated religious disestablishment, albeit out of somewhat different motives. Williams saw the dangers of state interference in the affairs of the church – the wilderness encroaching on the garden – while Jefferson recognized the dangers that religious interests and factions posed to the political order that he and the other founders had so carefully fashioned.

I should like to suggest, however, that the configuration of church and state embodied in the First Amendment – the guarantee of free exercise of religion and the proscription against religious establishment – has succeeded over the past two hundred years beyond even the boldest expectations of either Williams or Jefferson. This wall of separation – which more accurately resembles a line in the dust, continually drawn and redrawn – has satisfied Jefferson's concern that confessional agendas not disrupt political stability, and it has also ensured the religious vitality everywhere in evidence throughout American history.

One characteristic of the United States Constitution implicit in all the flummery and celebration that surrounded its bicentennial is the remarkable resiliency of that document forged in the heat of political debate and compromise two hundred years earlier. It is indeed an extraordinary achievement, a tribute not only to the ideas of James Harrington, John Locke, Common Sense Realism, and the example of such documents as the Union of Utrecht, but also to the daring and inventiveness of a group of politicians willing to build those ideas into a political structure that would hold thirteen disparate colonies to-gether.[12] The writers of the Constitution showed considerable pre-science in anticipating some of the problems that the new society might encounter – so much so, in fact, that a Supreme Court nomi-nee in the 1980s could claim that most contemporary legal disputes could be settled by simple recourse to the "original intent" of the framers – but they also crafted a document of great elasticity and adaptability.

The American form of government has endured for more than two hundred years, and that must surely be its singular achievement. But what lies at the heart of that stability? Surely the Constitution itself, with its checks and balances and its representative democracy, forms the foundation, later strengthened by the freedoms provided for in the Bill of Rights – the first ten Amendments – and by the enfranchise-ment of women and minorities.

The first clause of the First Amendment, with its guarantee of free exercise of religion and the proscription against religious establish-ment, has made a particular contribution to American political stabil-ity, I shall argue, because religious freedom has siphoned off social dis-content that might otherwise find expression in the political sphere. In other words, the kind of factionalism that concerned James Madi-son in *Federalist No. 10* more often than not has flourished in religion rather than politics, with the effect that some of the energy and dis-content that might be directed toward political change dissipates in re-ligious bickering. In that respect, the disestablishment of religion has not only reduced religious pressure on the state, it has also meant that religious factionalism has often provided a buffer against political rad-icalism.

The idea that religion upholds the temporal order and protects the prevailing political and cultural institutions is, of course, a com-mon refrain, repeated approvingly by Niccolo Machiavelli, Thomas Hobbes, Edmund Burke, and various Erastian Anglicans, and not so approvingly by Karl Marx and Friedrich Nietzsche.[13] The notion that religious *pluralism* can sustain the political order, however, is a uniquely American construct. Roger Williams and the founders of Rhode Island recognized the salutary effects of religious freedom. A "flourishing civil state may best be maintained," they believed, "with a full religious liberty, and . . . true piety will give the greatest security for sovereignty and true loyalty." [14] William Livingston, inveterate opponent of religious establishment in colonial New York, remarked in 1754 (a century later) that "nothing can tend so much to maintain our freedom and independency in religion as a division into a variety of sects." [15]

Not all American clerics recognized the value of disestablishment to religion immediately; some had to be converted. It was only after reflection that John Henry Livingston, a Dutch Reformed minister in New York, decided that in a country "where hearing is promoted & a spirit of enquiry prevails I am not apprehensive that the Christian religion can receive any essential injury from the greatest scope that can be given to religious freedom," adding that "forcing mankind into a union of sentiment by any machine of State is altogether preposterous & has done more harm to the cause of the gospel than the sword of persecution has ever effected." [16]

In New England, where Congregationalism enjoyed the benefits of establishment, the "standing order" of Congregationalist ministers at first bitterly opposed voluntarism, this notion that no one confession would enjoy preferential status, but they came in time to recognize the salutary effects of religious pluralism. Lyman Beecher initially lamented Connecticut's disestablishment of Congregationalism, in 1818, as "a time of great depression and suffering," but shortly thereafter, flushed with a general revival of religion, he changed his tune. "We were thrown on God and on ourselves, and this created that moral coercion which makes men work," he remembered in 1820. "Before we had been standing on what our fathers had done, but now we were obliged to develop all our energy." [17]

One of the striking features of the United States, as compared with other Western nations, is the steadfastly centrist nature of its politics. Whereas European nations, most of them governed through the parliamentary system, undergo periodic changes – new political parties, ever shifting coalitions – the two political parties in the United States cling tenaciously to the ideological center. The very difficulty of breaking the pattern of two-party alignment (witness the failed efforts of Ross Perot in 1992 and 1996, John B. Anderson in 1980, George Wallace in 1968, Henry A. Wallace in 1948, and Teddy Roosevelt in 1912) attests to the persistence of moderate politics. The United States has no Green Party to speak of, no Communist Party outside of Berkeley and Greenwich Village, no Conservative or Social Democratic Party that mounts a serious challenge to two-party hegemony.[18]

What America has, however, is religious diversity encompassing every conceivable tradition, confession, and ethnic group. The First Amendment gives all of them free rein. No religion is established, and no citizen is required to give allegiance (or monetary support) to any religious group.

And yet Americans do. The 1984 Gallup poll cited in the introduction found that only 9 percent of Americans expressed no religious preference. On the other hand, as noted previously, 56 percent claimed membership in a church or synagogue, and 40 percent said they attended church or synagogue weekly. Such figures are unheard of in England and Europe. In contrast, political participation is much higher there, while Americans are notoriously lackadaisical about exercising their right to vote. In Queens, New York, for instance, fewer than 55 percent of eligible voters are registered, and in the 1988 presidential election only 49.1 percent – less than half – of the voting-age population nationwide bothered to cast their ballots, a decrease from 53.1 percent in 1984.[19]

In America, then, religion rather than politics may provide the argot and the arena for popular discourse and the expression of discontent. The existence of what I've referred to as a kind of free market of religion, which means that citizen-consumers are free to shop in the unregulated "marketplace," also provides room for entrepreneurs. Anyone at all can gather around him or her a following of believers disenchanted in one way or another with the existing religious options. American history is full of examples: Alexander Campbell, Joseph Smith, Ellen Gould White, Mary Baker Eddy, Noble Drew Ali, J. Gresham Machen. The majority of popular religious movements, I believe, divert social discontent away from the political and into the religious sphere. As such, religion in America has usually served as a conservative political force – that is, its very existence as a safety valve for social discontent tends to protect the state from radical zealots and the paroxysms of revolution.

Indeed, religious sentiments freely subscribed to without the coercion of the government have often served to shore up mainstream political values and the claims of the state.[20] The *McGuffey Reader* of the nineteenth century, with its unabashed celebration of Protestant, middle-class, patriotic values, comes to mind, as do many other examples. The Catholic church in America, eager to shed its immigrant image, has gone out of its way to affirm the political order and to prove itself patriotic in spite of its putative loyalty to a foreign entity. Until recently, Reform Judaism required its rabbis to serve in the military chaplaincy. Most Protestants have taught their children and their congregants about the Christian's duty to the state as outlined in St. Paul's epistle to the Romans. Even the Mormons, after bitter disputes with the United States government in the nineteenth century, have become ardent defenders of the political status quo and a formidable conservative force.

The civil rights movement, deriving much of its energy and leadership from the black churches, was, in many respects, a *conservative* movement, at least in the means chosen to effect social change. Evangelicals, because of their populist theology and their genius at communication, have been particularly successful in the free marketplace of religion in America, and their reentry into the political arena in the mid-seventies – due in part to their contrived mythology about America's "Christian" origins – has helped to sustain a conservative swing in American politics.

Both American politicians and foreign observers have acknowledged the extent to which religious sentiment in America upholds the political order. In 1835, de Tocqueville reported that Americans believed a "sincere faith in their religion" was "indispensable to the maintenance of republican institutions," and he noted that "while the law permits the Americans to do what they please, religion prevents them from conceiving, and forbids them to commit, what is rash or unjust."[21] Extolling that connection has ever been a staple of political discourse. "Of all the dispositions and habits which lead to political prosperity," George Washington declared in his Farewell Address, "religion and morality are indispensable supports."[22] In the mid-twentieth century Dwight Eisenhower reasserted that symbiotic relationship bluntly. "Our government makes no sense unless it is founded on a deeply felt religious faith," he has been quoted as saying, "and I don't care what it is."[23]

I do not think there is any kind of mystical connection between religious conviction and the durability of America's political institutions, as de Tocqueville seems to imply. Rather, just as historians of an earlier age believed that the frontier served as a safety valve for social unrest or that a plenitude of wealth ensured a certain equilibrium,[24] I believe that the cornucopia of religious options – and the liberality with which Americans avail themselves of them – has contributed to America's political stability by providing an alternative to political dissent. It strikes me as no accident, for example, that the truly radical political movement of the sixties and early seventies, the student unrest directed against America's involvement in Vietnam, eventually dissipated in a wave of Eastern spirituality. Surely other forces – political, economic, and cultural – contributed as well, but I wonder if the plethora of religions in America, an abundance guaranteed by the First Amendment, did not help to deflect the radical impulses of the day.

Religious agendas do, of course, continue to shape our political debates, as they have always done. The identity of many Americans is tied up with their religious affiliations; many socialize almost exclusively within their religious groups and in any priority of self-disclosure would likely identify themselves as Lutheran or Catholic or Orthodox or Methodist before they would identify themselves as Republican or Democrat.

In 1855, Philip Schaff proposed that the religious verve and energy that he and other Europeans found in America could be traced to the voluntary principle, which, he said, "calls forth a mass of individual activity and interest among the laity in ecclesiastical affairs, in the founding of new churches and congregations, colleges and seminaries, in home and foreign missions, and in the promotion of all forms of Christian philanthropy." [25]

Schaff sought to vindicate his claim about the vitality of religion in America by comparing the patterns of religious affiliation in Berlin and New York City. "In Berlin there are hardly forty churches for a population of four hundred and fifty thousand, of whom, in spite of all the union of church and state, only some thirty thousand attend public worship," he wrote. "In New York, to a population of six hundred thousand, there are over two hundred and fifty well-attended churches, some of them quite costly and splendid, especially in Broadway and Fifth Avenue. In the city of Brooklyn, across the East River, the number of churches is still larger in proportion to the population, and in the country towns and villages, especially in New England, the houses of worship average one to every thousand, or frequently even five hundred, souls." And all of these, Schaff marveled, were supported not by public funds or state-enforced taxation, but by free-will offerings. [26] De Tocqueville had made a similar point twenty years earlier: "There are certain populations in Europe whose unbelief is only equaled by their ignorance and debasement," he wrote, "while in America one of the freest and most enlightened nations in the world fulfills all the outward duties of religion with fervor." [27]

The extraordinarily high level of religious belief and participation in America continues to confound Europeans today. By almost any standard, we are still a religious people. More than six Americans out of ten believe that "religion can answer all or most of today's problems," and only 10 percent express little or no confidence in organized religion.[28]

This confidence marks another distinctive characteristic of American religiosity – its lack of cynicism. Even with widespread publicity about the recent shenanigans of certain televangelists and the (sometimes disturbing, even tragic) activities of radical "cults," there seems to be very little anticlericalism – that is, animosity and suspicion toward religious leaders in general – in America today. Indeed, ever since the First Great Awakening, when evangelicals struggled bitterly against religious establishments and protested the European identification of the clergy with the aristocracy, American history has been virtually free of anticlericalism as such. This again derives, no doubt, from the availability of religious options guaranteed by the Constitution. Why put up with a minister, a confession, or a tradition not to your liking when there are so many alternatives for the taking? Religion has remained a force in America precisely because of this everchanging menu of religious entrées.

England, once again, provides a useful contrast. Recall, for instance, John Lennon's offhanded comment in 1966 that "Christianity will go" – that the Beatles were "more popular than Jesus now." In Britain that observation elicited nary a comment, but in America it triggered a wave of record burnings and anti–Beatles demonstrations across the country, the intensity of which made the young Liverpudlians fear for their lives.[29] Ironically, Lennon, a former chorister at St. Peter's Church in Woolton, was probably correct insofar as his observations applied to Britain. "We are not a very religious people anymore," a woman in London informed me during a recent visit, in a tone more bemused than apologetic, "and so we have tried to devise ways to use some of these old churches creatively." The parish church adjacent to the archbishop of Canterbury's London residence, just across the Thames from Parliament, is now a garden club. Over the past thirty years nearly 2,000 of England's 16,000 Anglican churches have closed for lack of use, and the established Church of England draws only about 3 percent of the population to its worship services.[30]

Perhaps after all the internecine religious battles of the Tudor and Stuart periods the English have simply wearied of religion, but I suspect that the relative absence of religious options in England has rendered Anglicanism rather bland and homogenized and that the English look elsewhere for their voluntary affiliations – to the plethora of political parties, for example, or to garden clubs.

Religious disestablishment and the guarantee of free exercise of religion in America, on the other hand, have provided the climate for a vigorous religious culture – one that is anything but bland or homogenized. Because various religious groups must compete to survive in a buyer's market, voluntarism has lent an unmistakably populist cast to religion in America. While an inevitable pandering to popular tastes has sometimes tended, I think, to elevate form over content and to diminish the overall quality of religious belief and commitment, religious freedom has also ensured a rich and variegated spiritual landscape. American religion boasts a diversity and vibrancy unmatched in any Western culture, and we Americans, with our passion for novelty and our notoriously latitudinarian religious beliefs, freely partake of this cornucopia.[31] And, of course, there is always the possibility that if you are dissatisfied with the available options, you can start your own religious group. The First Amendment guarantees that right.

Whereas historian Charles Beard has argued that the U.S. Constitution was a conservative document in that it safeguarded the economic interests of the landed elite, I am suggesting that the Constitution was conservative in a far more subtle way: the First Amendment, by setting up a free market of religion, has not only ensured religious vitality but it has also helped to thwart political radicalism by redirecting malcontents away from the structured public sphere of American politics and into the pliant and more private domain of religion.

Thomas Jefferson and Roger Williams make strange bedfellows, and it is easy to speculate on the issues upon which they would have disagreed. Williams – first a Puritan, then a Baptist, and then a "seeker" – held strict ideas about the importance of the Bible and the need to separate from evil. Jefferson, on the other hand, excised large portions of the Bible that failed to conform to his own rationalistic, Enlightenment notions. While Williams looked forward to a "never-ending harvest of inconceivable joys" in the afterlife,[32] Jefferson fervently believed that Americans would eventually embrace Unitarianism as their religion of choice.

Despite their radical differences in terms of theology, both Williams and Jefferson agreed on the desirability of religious disestablishment, Williams because he sought to maintain a pure church and Jefferson because he sought political stability. I would suggest that after two hundred years, both might take satisfaction in the results of the unprecedented experiment in religious toleration to which they each contributed. It has lent political stability by diverting social discontent into the religious sphere, and it has ensured religious vitality by guaranteeing untrammeled expression in the free marketplace of American religion.

It may be too much to assume of Roger Williams and Thomas Jefferson that either anticipated fully the effects of religious disestablishment in America. Most Americans are well aware of Jefferson's manifold contributions to American life – as architect and inventor, as political theorist, diplomat, and politician – while Williams remains a relatively obscure figure. "Why is our candle yet burning," Williams asked rhetorically near the end of his life, but to serve "God by serving the public in our generation?"[33] In insisting on freedom of religion and liberty of conscience, each of these leaders provided a service that extended well beyond his own generation.

CHAPTER THREE

Visions of Rapture

Optimism and Apocalypticism in American Culture

On the evening of Good Friday, 1878, Charles Taze Russell and a handful of followers, all clad in white robes, gathered at the Sixth Street Bridge in Pittsburgh to await the Millennial Dawn, their translation into heaven. His study of the Scriptures had convinced Russell, a haberdasher from Allegheny, Pennsylvania, that Christ had returned invisibly in 1874 and that now, three and a half years later, the Kingdom of God would begin and the faithful would be summoned to glory. It seems that their hopes were not realized. Russell later denied the incident (although Pittsburgh newspapers insisted otherwise), and he revised his theology to accommodate this disappointment. The Kingdom of Jehovah, he said, would begin in 1914, whereupon God and Satan would rule the world jointly until the Battle of Armageddon vanquished the forces of evil and inaugurated a theocratic millennium. (Russell, the founder of the Jehovah's Witnesses, later insisted that a spiritual transformation had indeed occurred in 1878. At that moment, he claimed, those among the elect who had died were raised into heaven, and thereafter any one of the elect still living in that year would not linger in the grave after death, but would be translated immediately into Christ's presence.) [1]

Almost half a century earlier, another self-educated student of the Bible named William Miller (formerly a farmer in Low Hampton, New York) calculated the date of Christ's return on the basis of the apocalyptic writings in the Bible, particularly the New Testament book of Revelation and the prophecies of Daniel in the Hebrew Bible (the Christian Old Testament). The 2,300 days until the cleansing of the temple, spoken of in Daniel 8:14, Miller insisted, should actually be taken as 2,300 years, beginning with the decree of Artaxerxes in 457 B.C.E. to rebuild Jerusalem. Simple arithmetic led him to pinpoint the year 1843 as the time of Christ's advent. In 1831, Miller began touring the Northeast with news of his discovery.

By Miller's own reckoning, he preached about 4,500 lectures to half a million people between 1831 and 1844.[2] Second Advent associations sprouted up in small towns all over the Northeast. In March 1840, the movement began publishing *Signs of the Times*, a monthly newspaper that eventually became a weekly. The organization also added a daily newspaper, *Midnight Cry*, a penny paper called the *Trumpet of Alarm*, another weekly called *Second Advent Harbinger*, and the *Voice of Elijah,* published by sympathizers in Montreal. A woman in Boston, Clarinda S. Minor, presided as editor of the *Advent Message to the Daughters of Zion*. Out West, the *Western Midnight Cry* emanated briefly from Cincinnati and *Glad Tidings of the Kingdom to Come* from Rochester, New York. In 1842, Millerites published their own hymnal, *Millennial Harp and Millennial Musings*.[3]

William Miller's followers did not rely on literature alone to disseminate their message. Prophetic charts proliferated, detailing Miller's calculations, illustrated with time lines, church ages, and the various beasts of Daniel and Revelation. Armed with three-by-six-foot banners, itinerant lecturers fanned out across the new nation to apprise audiences of the impending conclusion of human history and inform them of their peril unless they repented. Miller even took a page from the Methodists, the acknowledged masters at popular communication in the nineteenth century, and purchased what was reputedly the largest tent in America (one hundred and twenty yards in circumference with a fifty-five-foot center pole).[4]

As 1843 approached, anticipation and enthusiasm among Miller's fifty thousand followers reached a fever pitch. Preparations for the apocalypse had grown so pervasive that Horace Greeley published an "extra" edition of the *New-York Tribune* on March 2, 1843, to refute Miller's calculations. Pressed by his followers for a more precise date, Miller declared that the advent would occur sometime between

March 21, 1843, and March 21, 1844 (the Jewish year 5602). By May 2, 1844, Miller had acknowledged his error, but he urged his followers to remain vigilant. An associate later convinced him that he had failed to account for a "tarrying time," so Miller returned to his calculations and emerged with a new date for Christ's return, October 22, 1844.

Preparations resumed. While their crops remained unharvested and their stores shuttered, Millerites gave away their possessions and settled their accounts, both spiritual and temporal. Banks and financial agencies — even the United States Treasury, according to contemporary newspaper accounts — recorded large influxes of money to satisfy outstanding obligations. As October 22 dawned, Millerites gathered in their societies to await their elevation to glory. (According to some accounts — hotly denied by Adventists — some Millerites dressed in white muslin "ascension robes" waited in cemeteries.) But on October 23 they returned home, bitter and disappointed, to endure the mockery of their neighbors.[5] William Miller himself died lonely and forgotten in 1849, but the movement he inspired eventually regrouped after the Great Disappointment of 1844 and became known as the Seventh-Day Adventists. Today Miller's theological descendants claim a worldwide following well in excess of three million.[6]

Christians in general and American Protestants in particular have long evinced a fascination with the end of time and the role that they would play in the apocalypse foretold in the Bible. Indeed, Christopher Columbus invested the discovery of the New World with millennial significance. "God made me the messenger of the new heaven and the new earth of which he spoke in the Apocalypse of St. John [the book of Revelation] after having spoke of it through the mouth of Isaiah," Columbus wrote in 1500, "and he showed me the spot where to find it."[7]

More often, millenarian ideas have issued in the expectation that human history might screech to a halt at any moment and dissolve into some kind of apocalyptic judgment. These end-time notions, grounded in literalistic interpretations of biblical prophecies, admit of many different constructions, and evangelicals who agree on such issues as biblical inerrancy (that divine inspiration rendered the Scriptures without error in the original autographs) and church polity will argue bitterly over the specifics of those interpretations. Will God's elect go through the Tribulation – seven years of rule by the Antichrist, predicted in Revelation? Will the Rapture – Christ's return to summon the faithful, predicted in 1 Thessalonians 4 – occur before, during, or after the Tribulation?[8] Who or what is the Whore of Babylon described in Revelation 17? American Protestants have often settled on the Roman Catholic Church as a logical choice, but they have disagreed wildly on the identity of the Antichrist. Napoleon? The pope? Adolf Hitler? John Kennedy? Henry Kissinger? More recent speculation has centered around Ronald Wilson Reagan (because he has six letters in each of his three names, corresponding to the "mark of the beast," 666, foretold in Revelation 13:18), Mikhail Gorbachev (the birthmark on his forehead), or even Bill Gates (a rumor has circulated – appropriately enough, on the Internet – that if you assign ASCII numbers to the letters of his given name, they too total 666).

Will the millennium, one thousand years of godly rule on earth, take place before or after the Rapture? Has it already begun? The possibilities admit of many combinations: mid-trib premillennialists, post-trib postmillennialists, pre-trib premillennialists, and so on.[9] For three centuries now, columns of the faithful have mustered to wage these theological battles and to propagate what is certainly, they contend, the only possible construction of these obscure biblical passages.

Throughout American history, evangelicals have vacillated between pre- and postmillennialism. While the Puritans were decidedly premillennial in their views – that is, they knew that Christ's return could take place at any moment – the revivals of the Great Awakening of the 1730s and 1740s promoted a sense that God was even now working on earth to establish the millennial kingdom. No less a figure than Jonathan Edwards, regarded by many as one of America's premier intellects, believed that the millennium would begin in America.[10] The Society of Believers in Christ's Second Appearing, better known as the Shakers, held that Christ had already returned, in the person of Mother Ann Lee, and that they were busy establishing the millennial kingdom in the present. "The gospel of Christ's Second Appearing," according to the Shakers' Millennial Laws, "strictly forbids all private union between the two sexes, in any case, place, or under any circumstances, in doors or out." John Humphrey Noyes, founder of the Oneida Community in western New York, also believed that Christ had returned (in A.D. 70), but for him the millennium at hand allowed for sexual license in the form of "complex marriage."[11]

Postmillennialist language and imagery surfaced in various contexts throughout the eighteenth and nineteenth centuries. Many of the Patriots in the eighteenth century fused millennial expectations with radical Whig ideology and greeted the American Revolution as "the sacred cause of liberty."[12] While wandering through western Pennsylvania in 1779, Hermon Husband, a New Light evangelical, former North Carolina Regulator, and ardent antifederalist, came upon the eastern corner of the New Jerusalem. "I saw therein the Sea of Glass, the Situation of the Throne; which Sea was as clear as crystal Glass," Husband recalled. "I also saw the Trees of Life, yielding their monthly Fruit; and the Leaves of the Trees healing the Nations; one of which leaves I got hold of, and felt its healing Virtue to remove the Curse and Calamities of Mankind in this World."[13]

Amid the Second Great Awakening, at the turn of the nineteenth century, with all of America intoxicated with Arminian self-determinism, an air of optimism about the perfectibility both of humanity and society prevailed. Postmillennialism – the doctrine of Christ's triumphal reign on earth now – suited the mood, and it complemented nicely the Enlightenment's sanguine appraisal of human potential.[14] This spirit of optimism unleashed all manner of reform efforts – temperance, abolitionism, prison and educational reform, missions to the unconverted – consonant with the assurance that Christ was even then vanquishing the powers of evil and establishing his kingdom.[15]

Julia Ward Howe's "Battle Hymn of the Republic" popularized this triumphalism – the Kingdom of God as a juggernaut – during the Civil War:

> Mine eyes have seen the glory
> of the coming of the Lord:
> He is trampling out the vintage
> where the grapes of wrath are stored;
> He hath loosed the fateful lightning
> of his terrible swift sword:
> His truth is marching on.[16]

In only slightly more prosaic terms, the Reverend William Gaylord of Fitzwilliam, New Hampshire, echoed this sentiment. "Oh! what a day will that be for our beloved land, when carried through a baptism of fire and blood, struggling through a birth-night of terror and darkness, it shall experience a resurrection to a new life, and to a future whose coming glory already gilds the mountain tops," the Congregationalist minister said. "The day of the Lord is at hand!"[17]

Yet even in the heady days of evangelical reform and utopian idealism, in the first half of the nineteenth century, postmillennialism could not claim a monopoly on evangelical eschatology. Sobered by the excesses of the French Revolution, many evangelicals had tempered their optimism about the perfectibility of humanity and society and reverted to premillennialism. William Miller's adventist sentiments, for example, were unmistakably premillennial. Joseph Smith's apocalyptic notions led him in a slightly different direction. Convinced that the New Jerusalem would be centered in Jackson County, Missouri, Smith led a surveying party there, and on May 19, 1838, he staked out the holy city of Adam-ondi-Ahman. Persecution from neighbors and Smith's assassination in 1844 interrupted the preparations for the coming kingdom, but in recent years a small band of Mormons has returned to resume the task, to await the resurrection of Adam, the prophets, and church leaders, and the onset of the millennium.[18]

Among antebellum blacks, mired in slavery, apocalypticism took yet another form, a conviction that God sanctioned rebellion against white slaveholders, whose oppressions marked them for divine judgment. On May 12, 1828, God appeared to a slave preacher in Southampton County, Virginia, and, according to Nat Turner, "I heard a loud noise in the heavens, and the Spirit instantly appeared to me and said the Serpent was loosened, and Christ had laid down the yoke he had borne for the sins of men, and that I should take it on and fight against the Serpent, for the time was fast approaching when the first should be last and the last should be first." Thus emboldened, Turner unleashed his apocalypse on August 21, 1831, a rebellion that claimed the lives of fifty-five whites and two hundred blacks.[19] David Walker, a free black and a contemporary of Turner's, tried to sear the conscience of slaveholders with predictions of impending judgment: "O Americans! Americans!! I call God – I call angels – I call men, to witness, that your *DESTRUCTION is at hand*, and will be speedily consummated unless you *REPENT*."[20]

With some important exceptions, postmillennialism generally prevailed among American evangelicals until the latter half of the nineteenth century. In the decades following the Civil War, however, much of the optimism about society's perfectibility began to dissipate.[21] As the nation urbanized and industrialized, and waves of European immigrants, most of them Catholic, reached American shores, evangelicals lost their hegemony. Teeming, squalid cities and rapacious industrialists hardly looked like fixtures of a millennial kingdom. Society was not improving, becoming more Christian; it was degenerating, falling into enemy hands. America, moreover, began importing alien notions: Charles Darwin's theory of natural selection, which, pressed to its logical conclusions, undermined literal understandings of Scripture; and the German discipline of textual criticism, or higher criticism, which attacked the integrity of the Bible itself.

In the face of such degeneration, evangelical Christians began to revise their eschatology. Postmillennialism, with its optimism about the perfectibility of culture before the apocalypse, no longer fit, so American evangelicals cast about for an alternative, which they found in John Nelson Darby's dispensational premillennialism.[22] Darby, a member of the Plymouth Brethren in England, believed that all of history could be divided into seven dispensations and that the present age, "the age of the church," immediately preceded the Rapture of the church, the seven-year Tribulation, and the coming Kingdom of God.[23]

Darby's novel ideas, grounded in typology, numerology, and literalistic interpretations of the Bible, perfectly suited the temper of American evangelicals in the late nineteenth century. Instead of a society on a steady course of amelioration, they saw a society careening toward judgment. Increasingly pushed to the margins of American culture, evangelicals – many of whom became fundamentalists after the turn of the century – began to espouse a theology that looked toward the imminent return of Christ to claim his followers and prosecute his judgment against a sinful nation.

More often than not, this conviction prompted evangelicals to separate themselves from the corruption they saw everywhere around them. "I don't find any place where God says the world is to grow better and better, and that Christ is to have a spiritual reign on earth of a thousand years," the popular evangelist Dwight L. Moody declared confidently in 1877. "I find that the earth is to grow worse and worse, and that at length there is going to be a separation."[24] At the turn of the century, John Alexander Dowie, a pentecostal faith healer, attracted 7,500 followers to live in his utopian community, Zion City, Illinois, which he believed was the New Zion predicted in the book of Revelation and whose official incorporation in 1902 marked the beginning of another millennialist drama.[25] In some cases, especially early in the twentieth century, the rhetoric of evangelicals betrayed a thinly veiled contempt for the culture that they felt had spurned them. "It is a great thing to know that everything is going on according to God's schedule," William Pettingill told an audience of premillennialists in

1919. "We are not surprised at the present collapse of civilization; the Word of God told us all about it."[26]

As American culture and modernity itself seemed to turn increasingly hostile in the early decades of the twentieth century, evangelicals continued their retreat inward. Reeling from the ignominy of the Scopes trial in 1925, they immersed themselves in dispensational ideology, with its implicit condemnation of American culture. The Scofield Reference Bible, compiled by Cyrus Ingerson Scofield, provided a dispensational template through which evangelicals read the Scriptures. This Bible, first published by Oxford University Press in 1909, became enormously popular among evangelicals and fundamentalists and remains a strong seller, even though supplanted in some ways by an updated version, the Ryrie Study Bible, published in 1978.[27]

Premillennial sentiments and apocalyptic prophecies continue to inform evangelical views of the world. Sometimes they have political implications, such as unconditional support for the state of Israel, which evangelicals believe enjoys God's blessing and will play a critical role in the apocalypse.[28] Or consider the remark made before the House Interior Committee by James Watt, U.S. Secretary of the Interior from 1981 to 1983. "I do not know how many future generations we can count on before the Lord returns," he said, in an apparent attempt to rebut arguments for conserving natural resources.[29]

More often, however, apocalyptic convictions form the core of personal piety. Absorbed in the prophetic writings of the Bible, evangelical and fundamentalist preachers regularly exhort their congregations to prepare for the end, to repent and bring their neighbors to Christ. For most, it is not a matter of *if* Christ will return, but *when*. This "blessed hope" provides strength and succor while setting those who believe apart from a world that awaits judgment unknowingly. The words of an evangelical hymn, "This world is not my home / I'm just a-passing through," express both a discomfiture with the dominant culture and an expectation of a superior reward in the hereafter.[30]

How pervasive are these sentiments in American culture? Several indices, admittedly impressionistic and anecdotal, hint at the popularity of these ideas. In the late sixties and early seventies, Herbert W. Armstrong convinced many of his followers to surrender their assets to his Worldwide Church of God in anticipation of Christ's return in 1972. First published in 1970, *The Late Great Planet Earth*, which posits the imminent collapse of the world in apocalyptic judgment, has sold well over fifteen million copies; the *New York Times* named its author, Hal Lindsey, the best-selling author of the 1970s, and the book also inspired a movie by the same title, released in 1977 and narrated by Orson Welles.[31] Billy Graham, perhaps the most renowned of modern evangelists, shares similar premillennial views, a preoccupation suggested by the titles of two books he has written: *Till Armageddon* and *Approaching Hoofbeats: The Four Horsemen of the Apocalypse.*[32]

These examples only hint at the popular hold of millennial notions in American culture, and surely the fifteen million buyers of *The Late Great Planet Earth* included a generous sprinkling of the curious among the faithful. Yet for many in the evangelical subculture, apocalyptic imagery functions as a kind of vernacular, a common language of discourse, and they turn to the books of Daniel and Revelation to guide them through an increasingly perilous world.

Aside from their convictions about the literal truth of the Bible, evangelicals have many reasons for their fixation with the end of time. First, although this may seem improbable to those outside the evangelical subculture, it's a lot of fun. Evangelicals *enjoy* speculating about prophetic events. Just who *is* the Antichrist? Could those UPC codes in the supermarket someday be imbedded on the back of your hand for use as a kind of debit card, and would they thereby be the dreaded and pernicious mark of the beast? How do Desert Storm and the Persian Gulf War – battles in the vicinity of the Holy Land – fit into the prophetic scheme? Should true believers oppose the United Nations and the European Community as harbingers of the one-world government that some have predicted would facilitate the rise of the Antichrist? Some evangelicals thought the Orwellian year 1984 would herald the end of human history; later, similar predictions shifted to the year 2000. While it is true that all too often such speculations lead to paranoia and conspiracy theories, many discussions of this sort are rather innocuous.

Second, a preoccupation with the end times allows for flights of fancy about the shape of a new and perfect world, a chance to start over. In some instances, these visions about a new heaven and new earth have had a deleterious effect on evangelical engagements in this world: premillennialism has served to absolve believers from responsibility for social activism. Ever since the late nineteenth century, far too many evangelicals have retreated into a bunker mentality, reminding themselves that this world is getting worse, that the only hope is the imminent return of Jesus, and mollifying themselves with blueprints of the heavenly city.

A fixation on the prophecies in the Bible, moreover, places evangelicals in control of history. It allows them to assert that they alone understand the mind of God, they alone have unlocked the mysteries of the Scriptures. The corollary to this smugness, of course, is that everyone else is still benighted – lost in darkness and awaiting divine judgment – because they have refused to take the apocalyptic prophecies seriously.

Finally, and most importantly, evangelicals see the end times as a summons to conversion, and many pray fervently for a Third Great Awakening. We must set our lives and our hearts in order before Jesus returns, they insist, before it's too late. Is *my* heart right with God? What about family and loved ones? That's why the approach of the year 2000 excited both anticipation and anxiety among many evangelicals.

CHAPTER FOUR

A Pentecost of Politics

Evangelicals and Public Discourse

I could make my point by asking you to accompany me on a field trip. Our first stop would be the redoubtable neo-Gothic structure of St. Patrick's Cathedral on Fifth Avenue in New York City. There, at high mass on Sunday morning, as John Cardinal O'Connor stepped up to the pulpit, you might well be impressed by the sight of a real-life prelate – in living color, as the folks at NBC, just across the street in Rockefeller Center, used to say. Before long, however, your thoughts and your mind would wander. Your eyes would probably settle on the tourists walking past, who themselves would take only momentary notice of the bespeckled old man with a nasal drone in the funny costume, reading from a prepared text. And if I asked you twenty minutes after the service to recount for me the highlights of the cardinal's homily, I suspect that you would return the vacant stare of some hapless undergraduate who has just been asked to identify "dispensational premillennialism" on a mid-term examination.

Our second stop would be the True Bibleway Church of the Lord Jesus Christ of the Apostolic Faith in Natchez, Mississippi. The Sunday morning service has been going for two hours before Andre Ramsey steps to the pulpit. Pastor Elder Ramsey, as he is known to his congregation, is a self-educated man who supports himself as a lineman for the local utility company. He draws no salary whatsoever for serving as pastor of three churches in Mississippi, each of which he has built from scratch. You won't understand every word of Pastor Elder Ramsey's sermon, but you won't forget it either. And somewhere amid the jumping, the gesticulation, the frenzy, the pauses, and the ul-

ulation you recognize that this man may not be able to rehearse the teleological argument for the existence of God, but he knows how to communicate.

These are, admittedly, two extreme examples, but they illustrate the extent to which evangelicals understand the importance of communication. They have mastered the fine art of oral discourse, especially persuasive rhetoric, in a nation of talkers. I can think of no other culture so enamored of the human voice. We have talk radio and talk television, CB radios and cellular telephones. Letters, more often than not, are bills or legal documents or solicitations, not personal communications; we do that over the telephone.

The importance of the spoken word in America derives at least in part from Americans' disdain for tradition. In the religious arena Americans have always looked askance at creeds, formality, and liturgical rubrics. Indeed, the centrality of discourse – of preaching – in American evangelicalism is a direct legacy of the Protestant Reformation. Martin Luther understood the power of the spoken word to educate, to communicate, to mobilize. The extent to which evangelicals have appropriated that lesson is reflected in both their architecture and their orders of worship. In high-church traditions the altar is central, and the entire liturgy leads up to the Eucharist. In most evangelical churches, on the other hand, the pulpit is at center stage, and the service reaches its crescendo in the sermon, the spoken word. Throughout American history evangelical preachers have also regarded the sermon as a performance, a species of entertainment. George Whitefield, trained in the London theater, understood that no less than Lorenzo Dow, Billy Sunday, Jimmy Swaggart, or Robert Tilton.

The skill evangelicals display at popular communication – and the use of communications technology – is at odds with their image as somehow backwards or retrograde, and even a cursory review of American history suggests more than a casual connection between religious and political communications. As historian Harry Stout has pointed out, the persuasive rhetoric of evangelists during the Great Awakening provided a model for Patriot agitators during the Revolutionary era.[1] The communications networks that evangelicals established helped to knit together the thirteen disparate colonies. The Methodist circuit riders of the early nineteenth century brought evangelical religion to the frontier, and their organizational genius almost certainly provided the model for "grassroots" political organizations.

As Alexis de Tocqueville observed in 1835, the "two chief weapons which parties use in order to ensure success are the public press and the formation of associations."[2] No one understood both better than antebellum evangelicals, with their presses, their denominations, and their benevolent societies. The political devices of torchlight parades, tent meetings, and urgent calls for commitment, according to historian Daniel Walker Howe, were taken directly from revivalist preachers. National political conventions, whose purpose was to galvanize support and whip up enthusiasm, were copied from social reform organizations populated overwhelmingly by evangelicals.[3]

In the burgeoning cities of the United States in the latter half of the nineteenth century, political rallies mimicked the great urban crusades of Dwight Lyman Moody, J. Wilbur Chapman, and Billy Sunday, including their use of publicity, advertising, and prodigious advance work. In the early twentieth century, preachers like Charles Fuller and Aimee Semple McPherson were communicating their evangelical gospel over the radio airwaves a decade before Franklin Roosevelt discovered the radio as a political tool. And the televangelists of the 1970s used the emerging technology of satellite dishes and the deregulation of the airwaves to communicate their gospel on television well in advance of Ronald Reagan's masterful use of that medium for his own political ends.

Throughout American history, politicians have appropriated the language, the style, and the fervor of the preacher. Abraham Lincoln adopted the magisterial cadences of the King James Version of the Bible, and various preacher-politicians have risen to great heights of oratorical passion. Patrick Henry, who was influenced by the Presbyterian itinerant Samuel Davies, introduced evangelistic fervor, complete with histrionics and rhetorical flourishes, into the world of

Virginia politics.[4] The famous "Cross of Gold" speech by William Jennings Bryan, known as the "Great Commoner," was replete with religious imagery. Bryan's oratory electrified the Democratic National Convention in 1896, and perhaps it is no coincidence that when Bryan himself recalled that famous speech he remembered that in between the interruptions of tumultuous cheering "the room was as still as a church."[5]

In some cases, especially among African-Americans, the line between preacher and politician has been exceedingly vague, even nonexistent. Throughout American history, black preachers have served as oracles for their people on both religious and political matters. You need not like his politics to appreciate Jesse Jackson's oratorical artistry before the Democratic conventions of 1984 and 1988. Even though Jackson was not at the top of his form at the latter event in Atlanta, his performance provided a sharp contrast to the careful, measured delivery of his party's presidential nominee, Michael Dukakis.

The parallels between evangelical discourse and political rhetoric, furthermore, reach well beyond style. Relentless evangelical harangues directed against the settled clergy in the eighteenth century prefigured Revolutionary assaults on deference, privilege, and taxation without representation. The massive conversion of American Protestants from Calvinism to Arminianism in the early days of the Republic was no accident. Arminian theology, with its emphasis on the ability of individuals to control their own religious destinies, held considerable appeal for a people who had only recently taken up arms to achieve political independence. Those Calvinists who tried to block this democratization of theology were held up to ridicule. Peter Cartwright, for example, a Methodist revivalist during the Second Great Awakening, criticized "the old starched Presbyterian preachers" who opposed the revival.[6] In short, evangelical theology had to adjust to a people intoxicated with self-determinism, and the rhetoric of choice, individualism, and optimism pervaded both political and religious discourse throughout most of the period between the War of Independence and the Civil War. It is no coincidence, moreover, that the language of early-nineteenth-century millennialism tended more often than not to assign the United States a special place in the divine order.

Evangelical rhetoric in the decades following the Civil War was less optimistic, but it reflected, once again, the sentiments of many Americans – those who felt displaced and threatened by rapid urbanization, the incursion of non-Protestant immigrants (most of whom did not share evangelical scruples about temperance), and the corruption of big-city politics. In 1892, for instance, Charles H. Parkhurst, pastor of the Madison Square Presbyterian Church in New York City, unleashed a blistering attack against the Tammany Hall political machine and the police department, which he characterized as "a lying, perjured, rum-soaked and libidinous lot" who were "filthifying our entire municipal life, making New York a very hotbed of knavery, debauchery and bestiality."

Evangelical rhetoric in the twentieth century has been marked by dualism – us *versus* them, the righteous *versus* the unrighteous, America *versus* the world. Although evangelicals by and large had retreated from the public arena in the middle half of the twentieth century (from 1925 to 1975), their dualistic perspectives nevertheless fit quite comfortably with the political perpective of a nation engaged first in World Wars I and II, then in a "police action" in Korea, and finally in an unwinnable war in Indochina. Recall, for instance, Billy Sunday's "hang the Kaiser" rallies, and persistent evangelical denunciations of "godless Communism," which reached their apotheosis during the McCarthy era and only now show some signs of abating.

All of this suggests a correlation between evangelical rhetoric and public discourse. Throughout American history the relentless populism that has animated evangelicalism has both reflected and influenced the political and cultural currents of national life. Evangelical religion and American politics are so interconnected that the threads of causation are all but impossible to follow.

In religious terms this symbiosis has been a mixed blessing. At its best, it **has check**ed clerical arrogance and ensured at least a measure of religious accountability. At its worst, it has given rise to "wind-sock theology," an evangelicalism that shifts direction constantly according to the gusts of the larger culture. The shift from Calvinist to Arminian theology in the early Republic provides one such example. Another is the rise of prosperity theology in the 1980s, during the Reagan years. The self-aggrandizement, sybaritic leisure, and headlong quest for affluence that marked that decade found a theological legitimation of sorts in the tortured exegesis of those televangelists who promised jewelry, furs, vacation homes, and fancy automobiles to the faithful – all in the name of Jesus. This was evangelicalism's version of "trickle-down" economics. Prosperity in this case would trickle down from heaven, but it would reach the faithful, of course, only after it had cycled through the rain barrel of the televangelists.

The correlation between Reaganism and prosperity theology underscores yet another parallel between evangelicalism and the public arena, namely the relative absence of ideological ballast. Populist evangelical theology in America, like populist politics, operates on pragmatism more often than it does on principle. Put simply, neither can afford the luxury of ideological baggage. At an early stage in his career, Billy Graham turned aside a friend's challenge to attend Princeton Theological Seminary and become conversant with intellectual and theological issues. "I don't have the time, the inclination, or the set of mind to pursue them," Graham protested. "I have found that if I say, 'The Bible says' and 'God says,' I get results. I have decided I am not going to wrestle with these questions any longer."[7] Writing about American religion in 1855, Philip Schaff noted that in general Americans were active rather than contemplative, "more like the busy Martha than like the pensive Mary." American religion, he said, cannot claim "the substratum of a profound and spiritual theology."[8] Nor do American politics, in many cases, rest upon a secure ideological foundation.

Evangelicals, then, have shaped both the style and content of public discourse, and vice versa: evangelicalism alternately reflects and determines cultural trends. And if evangelicals generally have a knack for discerning the pulse of American popular sentiment, no figure in

American history has refined that sense better than the itinerant preacher, who not only provided a model for spreading the word (religious or political) but has also served as a kind of national bellwether.

In the eighteenth century, evangelical itinerants represented a threat to the established order. Puritanism in New England had collapsed beneath its own weight, but it left behind a state-supported, settled clergy that was increasingly jealous of its prerogatives. A similar situation obtained in the Middle Colonies and the Chesapeake, where the clergy hid behind the redoubts of either orthodoxy or ecclesiology or some combination of the two.

Itinerant preachers flushed them out, and in the process they helped to reshape American culture by unleashing a wholesale assault on clerical pretensions and complacency. Many of the clergy of the established denominations in the Middle Colonies had become ministers and immigrated from Europe to the New World in order to advance their social standing. What they faced instead was the obloquy of itinerants animated by evangelical Pietism. In the Raritan Valley, Theodorus Jacobus Frelinghuysen (though an immigrant himself, as we've noted) sounded a distinctly populist theme as he railed against the well-connected, orthodox clergy of New York — recall his pronouncement that "the largest portion of the faithful have been poor and of little account in the world."[9] Gilbert Tennent's famous sermon *The Danger of an Unconverted Ministry*, delivered at Nottingham, Pennsylvania, on March 8, 1740, and published later the same year, lamented the sinful condition of the colonial clergy and urged the faithful to seek their spiritual sustenance elsewhere. Similarly, John Henry Goetschius delivered himself of the view that "most of the ministers in this country were unregenerate ministers" and some "had already preached many people into hell." When called to account for his charges, Goetschius refused to acknowledge that ecclesiastical authorities had any jurisdiction over him and declared that those who opposed his peregrinations "were plainly godless people."[10]

The situation in New England was hardly more congenial to the enemies of evangelicalism. Itinerants like James Davenport, Timothy Allen, Benjamin Pomeroy, Eleazar Wheelock, Samuel Buell, and Andrew Croswell, among many others, directly challenged both the settled clergy and the standing order. "In Times past there hath been *Order* in the Churches of Christ, *instead of Religion*," Croswell wrote in 1742. "The Truth is, God never works *powerfully*, but Men cry out of *Disorder*: for God's *Order* differs vastly from their *nice* and *delicate* Apprehensions of it."[11] The more radical itinerants became the sworn enemies of order and decorum, and their assault culminated in the bonfires of the Shepherd's Tent, a New Light seminary in New London, Connecticut.[12]

How else did the colonial itinerants shape public discourse in the eighteenth century? With regard to form and technique, of course, they introduced extemporaneous preaching. The preeminent practitioner of this craft was George Whitefield, the "Grand Itinerant," who skillfully mixed evangelical rhetoric with dramatic devices that left his audiences awestruck. Whitefield's gift for oratorical persuasion is well documented by everyone from Nathan Cole, a Connecticut farmer, to Benjamin Franklin, no friend of organized religion, who, upon hearing Whitefield on Society Hill in Philadelphia, emptied his pockets to support Whitefield's orphanage in Georgia, despite his expressed skepticism about the wisdom of the enterprise. Whitefield and other eighteenth-century itinerants altered forever the character of religious and political discourse by emphasizing extemporaneous preaching and persuasive rhetoric, very much in contrast to the prevailing, more formal modes of address. Not only was this oratorical style crucial to the success of the Patriots in the Revolutionary era, the notion that the common people needed to be reached directly was both a precondition and an expression of egalitarianism.

There is a link here between the methods and the message of these eighteenth-century evangelists, whose challenge to the established order was not only theological but increasingly social and political as well. New Light Presbyterians and Baptist preachers undermined the gentility of colonial Virginia.[13] The "associated Pastors of Boston and Charles-Town" did not take kindly to James Davenport's practice of "going with his Friends singing thro' the Streets and High-Ways, to and from the Houses of Worship on Lord's-Days," inviting people to join him for prayer meetings *outside* of the churches. When Theophilus Pickering accused itinerant Nathaniel Rogers of behavior "subversive of the Order of the Gospel and Peace of the Churches" in 1742, he echoed the sentiments of scores of New England clergy.[14]

In some cases the clergy sought and obtained legal recourse against the itinerants, as when Connecticut threatened to banish them from the colony, but the itinerants flouted the laws and increasingly the populace supported them. When the prospect arose that the Church of England might send a bishop to the American colonies, William Livingston of New York worried publicly about the "ambitious designs" of such a prelate, and many colonists came to regard the Anglican bishop as yet another example of British imperialism and a threat to American liberties.[15] The rhetoric of liberty from ecclesiastical constraints melded almost seamlessly into the language of liberty from political oppression.

The itinerants of the eighteenth century brazenly challenged ecclesiastical hierarchies; their machinations divided churches into revivalist and antirevivalist camps and laid the groundwork for the proliferation of sectarianism in America. Mendicant preachers rent what was left of the unified social fabric in New England by placing revivalist preachers and congregations in competition with the established or "standing order" churches. And in time the evangelical "separates" allied with Enlightenment deists to press for disestablishment in the new nation.

Because of the disestablishment of religion mandated by the First Amendment, the term "dissenter," applied so liberally to itinerants in eighteenth-century New England, had little resonance in the early years of the Republic. Mendicant preachers performed a very different function in the early decades of the nineteenth century than they had in the eighteenth. Whereas once they had *disrupted* the social order, now they *brought* social order to many parts of the new nation. Evangelical itinerants tamed some of the rowdiness of life on the frontier, for instance, where lawlessness, alcohol abuse, and violence were rampant.

Once again, and importantly, the message of the itinerants was populist – simple, easy to understand, and delivered extemporaneously. In his autobiography, Richard Allen, founder of the African Methodist Episcopal Church, spoke for many others when he identified the Methodists as the primary oracles of evangelicalism among African-Americans. "We are beholden to the Methodists, under God, for the light of the Gospel we enjoy; for all other denominations preached so high-flown that we were not able to comprehend their doctrine," Allen wrote. "Sure am I that reading sermons will never prove so beneficial to the colored people as spiritual or extempore preaching."[16]

The most spectacular showcase for extemporaneous preaching in the antebellum period was the camp meeting, which attracted both settlers and itinerants from long distances. Evangelical preachers, using the language of the vernacular, attacked and ridiculed Calvinist theology for its elitism. As historian Nathan Hatch has argued, religion in the early Republic – be it that of Methodism, the Baptists, the Disciples of Christ, the black churches, or Mormonism – was doggedly democratic in spirit and populist in tone, much to the chagrin of the elite classes. Samuel Goodrich, editor of Boston's first daily newspaper, described one of these preachers, "Crazy" Lorenzo Dow, as "uncouth in his person and appearance." "It is scarcely possible to conceive of a person more entirely destitute of all natural eloquence," Goodrich wrote. "But he understood common life, and especially vulgar life – its tastes, prejudices and weaknesses; and he possessed a cunning knack of adapting his discourses to such audiences."[17]

Antebellum itinerants brought a distinctly evangelical version of civilization to the frontier. "We had no pewed churches, no choirs, no organs," Peter Cartwright recalled wistfully in 1856. "The Methodists in that early day dressed plain; attended their meetings faithfully, especially preaching, prayer and class meetings; they wore no jewelry, no ruffles."[18]

The itinerant preacher, traveling alone, became a kind of paradigm of the particularly American individualism that was also embodied in Jacksonian democracy. He (and sometimes she) harbored a disregard – even a disdain – for ecclesiastical hierarchies and authorities, and for pretension of any sort. During this period, itinerants and their evangelical theology served as a democratic and leveling force: women exhorted in revival meetings; female abolitionists appeared before "mixed audiences" of women and men; slave preachers addressed white congregations.

As the nineteenth century wore on, the expanding nation was convulsed by social, economic, and demographic changes, and the evangelical itinerant riding on horseback became the colporteur riding the Iron Horse. Methodist minister John Wesley Osborne was one of many circuit riders who made that transition directly, becoming a traveling peddler of religious materials for the American Tract Society in 1851.[19] And, like the circuit riders of the Jacksonian era, the new religious itinerants depended upon individualism. The entire colporteur scheme, according to the Society, combined "two of the mightiest elements of influence over the human mind . . . *individual christian example and effort, and a sanctified press.*"[20]

The American Tract Society itself traced the practice of distributing Bibles and literature to the Reformation of the sixteenth century and even to the apostles, the original evangelists. "Such is *the vastness of the country* as to require, especially in the newer States, an itinerant system of evangelization," the Society wrote in 1836.[21] The United States needed schools, colleges, and seminaries, the Society declared – "ministers must be multiplied" – and the colporteur system, which exploited new means of travel and new technology, offered unique advantages as well as immediate results. The progress of the gospel in the nineteenth century necessitated "an agency that is truly republican – going as the colporteur does to *all the people*, and first of all to those to whom no one else goes, with means of light and salvation." Above all, the Society's rhetoric was democratic: "If we would ignite a mass of anthracite, we must place the kindling at the bottom: if we would kindle the fire of knowledge and piety, we must commence at the lowest point of social being."[22]

Colporteurs not only sold Bibles, in the course of their peregrinations they performed marriages, served various missionary functions, set up lending libraries in the "public rooms" of hotels, organized Sunday schools, and preached to various congregations, including those gathered at railroad stations. Once again, evangelicals brought their message to the people. During an era when political campaigns were also conducted by rail, Osborne, for instance, traveled over twenty thousand miles in his first year as a colporteur on the Illinois Central Railroad, distributing Bibles, counseling travelers, and forging friendships with porters and conductors.[23]

What was the colporteur's relationship to the larger culture? The Bible peddlers took full advantage of the national rise in literacy, and they also functioned as harbingers of the emerging commercial economy and the culture of consumption.

The early literature of the American Tract Society had placed a great deal of emphasis on the need to *distribute* Bibles – to sell them, if possible, but to give them away if need be. While the *Instructions of the Executive Committee of the American Tract Society, to Colporteurs and Agents*, published several decades later, in 1868, did not disregard altogether the importance of propagating the gospel, the tone had shifted somewhat: "Though strictly a benevolent enterprise, there are endless details of a business character, requiring as much accuracy and care as in mercantile or banking transactions." The Society's New York office supplied two account books to every colporteur, together with detailed instructions about bookkeeping: "As far as possible, fill every blank."[24]

The Society also offered advice on sales techniques. "In effecting sales, there will be occasion for all your skill and talent," the *Instructions* stated. "The merchant is unwearied in bringing forward articles to attract the purchaser. . . . Endeavor to secure attention to the contents, character, and usefulness of the books, before asking the family to purchase." The Society urged its colporteurs to exhibit their entire line of goods, and it understood the importance of packaging and merchandising: "Be careful to call attention to the publications for children and youth, which are so beautifully printed and illustrated by engravings so as to tempt every eye, and so rich in spiritual instruction to profit every heart."[25] In the emerging consumer society of the late nineteenth century, the minister had, in effect, become a merchant.

By the early decades of the twentieth century, other evangelical itinerants of the day – the urban revivalists – had also adopted the language of commerce. Billy Sunday, a former baseball player for the Chicago White Stockings, began his evangelistic career barnstorming through the Midwest. After 1912, Sunday took his rallies to the cities, where he promised business and civic leaders that he could revive the churches, end labor unrest, and close the saloons – all for two dollars a head. As historian Douglas Frank has noted, Sunday, who once declared that he would stand on his head in a mud puddle "if I thought it would help me win souls to Christ," combined personal charisma, colloquial language, and vaudeville antics with an astute business sense. Within a culture that was becoming enamored of statistics, success for Billy Sunday was measured in numbers – attendance at the services, number of converts, total cost of the event. Advertising campaigns, careful planning, and prodigious advance work marked Sunday's campaigns.[26]

The irrepressible Aimee Semple McPherson was another of the early-twentieth-century evangelicals who understood the prevailing mood of the culture. Like thousands of itinerant preachers before her, Sister Aimee tirelessly toured the country, and, in an age when the motor car was very much a novelty, she knew how to attract attention. McPherson decorated her "Gospel Auto" with evangelistic slogans and once drove it in a Mardi Gras parade. After she settled in Los Angeles, McPherson's show-business antics rivaled those of Hollywood, across town. Her standard uniform consisted of a white dress, a blue cape, and a bouquet of red roses (the red-white-and-blue of patriotism), suggesting that she was playing out her childhood ambition of becoming an actress. On one occasion she rode onto the stage of Angelus Temple astride a motorcycle, and on another she delivered her sermon dressed in yellow, from the plaster-of-paris petals of a giant Easter lily. [27]

In 1922, McPherson became the first woman to preach a sermon over the radio. Shortly thereafter, Angelus Temple established the first religious radio station, KFSG, thereby heralding yet another – perhaps the final – chapter in the history of evangelical itinerancy. The use of the media in the twentieth century by evangelical leaders – both radio and television, and now the Internet – has solved forever the problem of reaching the people because it allows the evangelist, in effect, to be everywhere at once. Evangelical preachers from McPherson to Marilyn Hickey, from Charles Fuller and Billy Graham to Jerry Falwell and Frederick Price, have taken full advantage of the latest in communications technology. Whereas early in the nineteenth century, Methodist circuit riders braved the elements to bring the gospel to the frontier, the radio evangelists of the 1920s and 1930s and the televangelists of the 1970s and 1980s could address the masses from the comfort of a studio.

How has this latest development affected public discourse? Every election year political pundits decry the vacuousness of American political rhetoric, implying that in some long-forgotten halcyon age every matter of public interest was debated fully, intelligently, and without caricature. Indeed, there can be little doubt that the electronic media, television especially, have often compromised the quality of public discourse, if for no other reason than that these media are not (as yet) interactive. The cheapening of discourse, this pandering to the lowest common denominator, applies equally to religion and to politics.

But I wonder if there is anything novel about this. American rhetoric, whether religious or political, has often featured style rather than substance. After Bryan's stirring speech on the floor of the Democratic convention in 1896, John Peter Altgeld, governor of Illinois, called it "the greatest speech I've ever listened to" but soon thereafter asked a friend, "What did he say anyhow?"[28] Millions of auditors throughout American history can attest to the same confusion following an evangelical sermon or a political speech.

The close relationship between political discourse and evangelical rhetoric in particular, however, ensures a continued emphasis on style *over* substance. The absence of religious hierarchies in American evangelicalism has given rise to the cult of personality. Evangelicals, for the most part, do not organize themselves into churches according to creeds or doctrines, or even polity; they come together instead around a charismatic leader. Television has only exaggerated this tendency, but it is no less present in politics, especially with the breakdown of grassroots political organizations over the last quarter century. The cult of personality is pervasive in both evangelical religion and American politics. Popular success in America depends on one's ability to galvanize a following, be it a congregation or a constituency.

In the United States one of the most reliable ways to do that is to rehearse democratic, populist themes – to rail against pretension and the entrenched elite, whether the latter be an imperial presidency or a bishop dressed in ecclesiastical finery. The signal contribution of itinerants to American life is the remarkable absence of anticlericalism in the United States. Itinerant preachers also helped to ensure the absence of anticlericalism in a more direct way: their perorations against elitism and arrogance forced ministers to adopt a popular idiom, both in message and in comportment. Successful politicians have echoed those populist themes, sometimes disingenuously, to be sure, but effectively nonetheless.

The line between the preacher and the politician in American culture, both in style and in substance, is indeed a thin one. Pastor Elder Ramsey, summoning his congregation to Jesus with his extemporaneous delivery and his religious egalitarianism, has a great deal in common with the stump politician casting for votes. Both understand the value of entertainment, the force of persuasion, and the importance of aligning themselves – rhetorically, at least – against the privileged, the powerful, and the pretentious.

The symbiotic relationship between evangelicalism and public discourse has given both a distinctly populist cast and has led to a melding of styles. Perhaps an anonymous woman from Kansas captured this connection best when she described the 1890 political campaign as "a religious revival, a crusade, a pentecost of politics." [29]

CHAPTER FIVE

A Loftier Position

American Evangelicalism and the Ideal of Femininity

No issue has caused evangelicals more consternation in the second half of the twentieth century than feminism. The campaign for women's suffrage had led to the passage and ratification of the Nineteenth Amendment, granting women the right to vote, in 1920. In 1963, the publication of *The Feminine Mystique*, by Betty Friedan, heralded a new women's movement, one which would bring radical changes in gender roles, economic expectations, sexual behavior, the composition of families, and even in language. In 1945, the number of American women in the labor force stood at 29 percent; by 1970 that number had risen to 38 percent, and in 1995 to 46 percent. [1]

Among evangelicals, the response to the emergence of feminism and the push for equal rights for women has been both curious and ironic. On the face of it, evangelicals should have embraced feminism – indeed, they should have led the movement; after all, their forebears early in the nineteenth century were in the vanguard of pushing for gender equality and women's suffrage. Some of the most important leaders of nineteenth- and early-twentieth-century evangelicalism were women. Instead of adding their voices to the feminist cause, however, in the late twentieth century many evangelicals went through all manner of contortions to oppose it, first by clinging to the nineteenth-century cultural ideal of femininity, with its exaltation of female piety as the purest expression of Christianity, and then by lending their support to such organizations as the Promise Keepers, a mass movement of evangelical men in the 1990s.

During a 1989 television interview, Bailey Smith, an evangelical and an official of the Southern Baptist Convention, offered his view on women. "The highest form of God's creation," he said, "is womankind."[2]

Such pronouncements have become so commonplace among American evangelicals late in the twentieth century that it is easy to gloss over their significance. Those who purported to be the guardians of Christian morality, a tradition that more often than not has blamed Eve for Adam's downfall, trumpeted the unique purity of women, the "highest form of God's creation."

A particular kind of idealization of women permeates evangelical piety. If you page through any evangelical songbook published after, say, 1840, you will find all sorts of examples of women alternately praying and weeping for their children, waiting for wayward, sometimes drunken, sons to come home. "Tell Mother I'll be There," for instance, is a forlorn, anguished cry from one such son, who wants desperately to assure his mother, now "home with Jesus," that her prayers have been answered, that he has reformed. Paeans to female goodness and piety intensify as Mother's Day approaches each year.

> Mother is the sweetest word
> You and I have ever heard!
> Mother, oh how dear the thought,
> A bit of heaven you have brought![3]

All of this might be dismissed merely as vulgar sentimentality, the Protestant counterpart to popular Catholic pinings for the Virgin Mary, but the celebration of female piety by evangelicals has a particular focus in the home. If the Blessed Virgin ever sorted socks, scrubbed the kitchen floor, or worried about ring-around-the-collar, we seldom hear about it, even from her most devoted followers.

Not so for evangelical women. Their identity is tied almost exclusively to motherhood and to what one evangelical writer has called "the oft-maligned delights of homemaking."[4] You do not have to look very far in evangelical literature to find celebrations of motherhood and female domesticity. "Raising children is a blessing from the Lord, and I can't imagine a home without the mother being there," Nancy Tucker, a "stay-at-home mother," wrote in the evangelical magazine *Focus on the Family*.[5] "Being a mother, and filling mother's place, is one of the greatest responsibilities there is in this . . . world," an editorial in *The Way of Truth* proclaimed. "Those who feel that a woman is wasting her time, and burying her talents, in being a wife and mother in the home, are simply blinded by the 'gods' of this world." Such domestic duties, the editorial continued, must not be taken lightly.

> What a grave and sacred responsibility this is. To provide food, clothing and shelter, may be the easiest part for many couples. To be a true *mother* goes far beyond supplying these temporal needs. The love, the nurturing, the careful guiding, the moral example, the moral teaching, the training, is the most important of all.[6]

An article in *Kindred Spirit*, a magazine published by Dallas Theological Seminary, echoes this theme. "In many ways God measures a woman's success by her relationship with her husband and children," the author, a woman, writes. "Many women ache to learn how to be truly successful in marriage and motherhood."[7]

This ideology, of course, is cloaked in biblical literalism. The apostle Paul is not usually remembered as a feminist, and evangelicals generally refuse to see his proscriptions as culturally conditioned. While most evangelicals have maneuvered around Paul's insistence that women keep their heads covered in church, they cannot see—or have elected *not* to see—his commands to women to keep silence and to be submissive as similarly culture-bound. Consequently, evangelical women are expected to be submissive, to demand no voice of authority in the church or in the home. As the article in *Kindred Spirit* puts it,

> Young women need to be taught a biblical view of their roles and relationships with their husbands in order to truly liberate them to be all that God intended them to be and to experience the best that He has for them.[8]

Paradoxically, then, evangelical women are supposed to feel a kind of liberation in this submission to their husbands.[9] "In seeking to recognize the crucial role of the husband and father as head of the household," the argument goes, "perhaps we have lost sight of the ways that family warmth is generated by the love and security given by a godly wife and mother."[10]

It was not always thus in American history, even in the evangelical tradition. I have already alluded to the discrepancies between certain historic elements of Christian theology and the contemporary idealization of women by evangelicals. Through the centuries, Christian theology has often regarded women as temptresses, the descendants of Eve, the inheritors of a wicked, seductive sensuality that could be tempered only through their subordination to men. John Robinson, pastor of the Pilgrims in Plymouth, Massachusetts, for instance, enjoined a "reverend subjection" of the wife to her husband, adding that she must not "shake off the bond of submission, but must bear patiently the burden, which God hath laid upon the daughters of Eve."[11] The Puritans of New England also harbored traditional suspicions about women: consider their treatment of Anne Hutchinson, their contempt for the Quakers' egalitarian attitude toward women, and the evident misogyny of the hysteria surrounding the Salem witch trials. Cotton Mather, the redoubtable Puritan divine, referred to women as "the hidden ones," a phrase betraying his misgivings about female spirituality. More important, the Puritans regarded the man as both head of the household and the person responsible for the spiritual nurture and welfare of his children.

Around the turn of the eighteenth century, however, a change in religious rhetoric signaled a shift in sentiment in New England. Women, who joined the churches in far greater numbers than men, began to be extolled as uniquely tender and loving and hence spiritually superior to their husbands, who were increasingly involved in commercial pursuits.[12] Whereas during the Revolutionary era "virtue" was a political term, applied to the fusion of civic humanism with evangelical ardor, by the end of the eighteenth century the word had become synonymous with femininity. [13]

The nineteenth century witnessed a revolution in domestic life in America, with the romanticization of the home, changes in gender roles, and, finally, the idealization of female piety. While there is some evidence that the republican ideals of the Revolutionary era permeated family life and led, at least for a time, to a relative equality of husbands and wives, the real changes occurred during the Second Great Awakening, early in the nineteenth century, when women were freed from institutional restraints in the enthusiasm of the revival. [14] The Second Awakening taught that everyone was equal before God, a notion that combined roughly equal parts of republican ideology and Arminian theology, which emphasized the ability of individuals to initiate the salvation process. Charles Grandison Finney's "new measures," moreover, encouraged women's participation in revival meetings, and evangelical women began to assert themselves as leaders of various benevolent and social reform movements. [15] Some women, such as Phoebe Palmer, Sarah Lankford, and Margaret (Maggie) Van Cott, became influential evangelists during this period.

Despite the temporary loosening of restraints during times of revival, nineteenth-century women rarely ascended to positions of religious authority. Whenever evangelical women aspired to leadership they were met with stern warnings or gentle but firm admonitions. Presbyterian minister Ashbel Green, sometime president of the College of New Jersey, reminded his auditors in 1825 that Christ framed women "with that shrinking delicacy of temperament and feeling, which is one of their best distinctions, which renders them amiable." He acknowledged that such feminine delicacy, "while it unfits them for command" and "subjects them, in a degree, to the rougher sex, gives them, at the same time, an appropriate and very powerful influence." Green concluded that women could not, however, expect that Christ "who formed them with this natural and retiring modesty, and under a qualified subjection to men, would ever require, or even permit them, to do anything in violation of his own order." [16]

Did this mean that women had no spiritual role to play whatsoever? On the contrary, according to Green and his colleagues, women must assume responsibility for the home and in particular for the spiritual nurture of the children. "The female breast is the natural soil of Christianity," Benjamin Rush, a fervent evangelical, opined.[17] "It is one of the peculiar and most important duties of Christian women," Green wrote, "to instruct and pray with children, and to endeavor to form their tender minds to piety, intelligence, and virtue."[18] Here was the proper sphere of female spirituality – as moral guardians of the home, in charge of the religious instruction and nurture of the children. "The family state," Catharine Beecher and Harriet Beecher Stowe wrote in 1869, "is the aptest earthly illustration of the heavenly kingdom, and in it woman is its chief minister."[19]

This idea of women as spiritual titans was new in the nineteenth century and peculiar to America. "Although the women of the United States are confined within the narrow circle of domestic life, and their situation is in some respects one of complete dependence," Alexis de Tocqueville wrote in 1835, "I have nowhere seen woman occupying a loftier position." After outlining Americans' distinctive and careful division of "the duties of man from those of woman," de Tocqueville attributed America's "singular prosperity and growing strength" to "the superiority of their women."[20]

Feminist scholar Ann Douglas calls this development the "feminization of American culture," and argues that it was the product of a collusion between nineteenth-century clergy, whose power and status were waning, and housewives eager for some emotional outlet.[21] Men came to be characterized as aggressive and indifferent to godliness, whereas women became the lifeblood of the churches. They were the repositories of virtue, meek and submissive – like Jesus himself. Thus, female spirituality was upheld as an ideal, a notion taken to its extremes in Shaker theology and even in Christian Science, both of which asserted explicitly the superiority of the feminine and linked the perfection of humanity to womanhood.

Women, therefore, came to be seen – and to see themselves – as responsible for the inculcation of virtue into their daughters, sons, and husbands. The evangelical women of Utica, New York, for instance, organized themselves into a Maternal Association that met biweekly and required that each member pledge to pray for her children daily, to read literature on Christian child-rearing, to set a pious example, and to spend the anniversary of each child's birth in fasting and prayer.[22]

Other forces besides revivalism lay behind this transition from the spiritual patriarchy of the Puritan family to the evangelical household of the nineteenth century. The early Republic witnessed the gradual emergence of a market economy and the stirrings of nascent industrialization. Men began to work outside the home and off the farm. They eventually organized into guilds as their labor became increasingly specialized. Traditional family and kinship networks gave way to associations among fellow workers. Families were no longer self-sufficient; they depended on the wages of men. Gender roles became more distinct. "From the numerous avocations to which a professional life exposes gentlemen in America from their families," Benjamin Rush, a physician and a signer of the Declaration of Independence, wrote, "a principal share of the instruction of children naturally devolves upon the women."[23] Men increasingly distanced themselves from domestic chores and activities, and women succumbed to the "cult of domesticity" or the "cult of true womanhood," marked by purity, piety, and devotion to family and household.

Thus sentimentalized, women assumed responsibility for domestic life, especially the religious instruction of the children. For many, in fact, the two were inseparable. In his *Treatise on Bread, and Bread-Making*, temperance lecturer and health reformer Sylvester Graham explicitly assigned to mothers the responsibility for both the physical and moral well-being of their children. It is the mother, wrote Graham, "who rightly perceives the relations between the dietetic habits and physical and moral condition of her loved ones, and justly appreciates the importance of good bread to their physical and moral welfare."[24]

Indeed, the sphere of domesticity – including the home, education and nurture of children, and religious matters generally – was the one area where the nineteenth-century woman reigned supreme, her judgments largely unchallenged. "In matters pertaining to the education of their children, in the selection and support of a clergyman, and in all benevolent enterprises, and in all questions relating to morals or manners, they have a superior influence," Catharine Beecher wrote in *A Treatise on Domestic Economy* in 1841. "In all such concerns, it would be impossible to carry a point, contrary to their judgement and feelings; while an enterprise, sustained by them, will seldom fail of success."[25]

An important theological development – a new focus on religious instruction and socialization – also reinforced the importance of female nurture. Early in the nineteenth century, the tides of revival swept away strict Calvinist doctrines of original sin and humanity's inherent depravity, emphasizing instead the ability of the individual to control his or her spiritual destiny; eventually this undermined the traditional emphasis on dramatic conversions. Indeed, Horace Bushnell's *Christian Nurture*, published in 1847, insisted that children should be reared from birth as though they were Christians, that parents should not expect a dramatic conversion experience in their children. Rather, children should be educated and socialized in such a way that they would always consider themselves Christian, or, in Puritan terms, among the elect. Who should perform this duty, especially in a society with increasingly differentiated gender roles? With fathers away at the mill or the factory all day, the task of "Christian nurture" fell to women.

To an ever greater extent, the home thus became the women's sphere, one which both defined and delimited female influence. As the Victorian era unfolded, moreover, mechanized production and a commercial economy increasingly eased domestic burdens, especially for the middle-class mother, who very often had a "hired girl" (usually a recent immigrant) to help with household chores. No longer must a middle-class woman spend her hours sewing, weaving, making soap, or butchering meat for her home. Instead, her husband's wages and the commercial economy gave her time to fuss over it. A passel of magazines, such as *Godey's Lady's Book*, instructed the Victorian woman on how to decorate her home with ornate woodworking and carvings and a vast array of furnishings – bookcases, clocks, over-stuffed chairs – now within her budget. The invention of the power loom in 1848 made carpets plentiful and affordable. The parlor organ became a kind of domestic shrine, with its high verticality, its carved, pointed arches, and its nooks, crannies, and shelves for family photographs and mementos. The organ itself, used for family hymn-singing, both symbolized and reinforced religious notions and the ideal of feminine domesticity: *Mother* played the organ and thereby cemented her role as the religious keystone of the family.[26]

These notions about feminine spirituality and the role of women have persisted among evangelicals in the twentieth century. Many of the taboos devised by evangelicals in their time of beleaguerment in the 1920s and 1930s centered around women. In reaction to the perceived moral laxity of a larger culture that was (in their view) careening stubbornly toward judgment, fundamentalists insisted that women forswear worldly adornments, especially jewelry and cosmetics. They devised elaborate parietal rules intended to protect the sexual innocence of their children, especially the girls, who were perceived as vulnerable to the animal cravings of less-spiritual males.

The Victorian myth of feminine spiritual superiority became so entrenched that many preachers felt obliged to counter it.[27] Recall, for instance, the machismo posturings of evangelist Billy Sunday, who insisted that in Jesus we find "the definition of manhood."[28] "God is a masculine God," the firebrand John R. Rice insisted to a male audience in 1947. "God bless women, but He never intended any preacher to be run by a bunch of women."[29] But the intensity of Rice's protestations merely verifies the pervasiveness of the myth. Presbyterian preacher Donald Grey Barnhouse confirmed this in his characterization of a typical Christian household. "The husband is not interested in the things of God, so the family drifts along without any spiritual cohesion," he wrote. "Perhaps they all go to church together on Sunday morning, and the wife goes to all the activities of the week, but the husband seems uninterested." Barnhouse then offered a familiar, albeit paradoxical, prescription for this malaise: feminine submission. "With delight she learns the joy of knowing it is her husband's house, his home; the children are his; she is his wife," he wrote. "When a woman realizes and acknowledges this, the life of the home can be transformed, and the life of her husband also." [30]

This notion reached its apotheosis in the 1970s with the enormous popularity of Marabel Morgan's book *The Total Woman*. The answer to a troubled marriage, Morgan preached, lay in becoming a "Total Woman," a wife who submitted abjectly to her husband and who burrowed herself ever deeper into the putative bliss of domesticity. "A Total Woman caters to her man's special quirks, whether it be in salads, sex, or sports," Morgan wrote. "She makes his home a haven, a place to which he can run." [31]

Given their investment in this ideal of feminine domesticity, it is no wonder that evangelicals found the larger society's rapidly changing views of women in the latter half of the twentieth century utterly disconcerting. Perhaps nothing – not even Darwinism and higher criticism, the burning issues of the 1910s and 1920s – so contributed to their sense of cultural dislocation. American evangelicals were caught off guard by *The Feminine Mystique*, and the ensuing feminist movement left them confused and full of resentment because the domestic ideal that fundamentalism had reified since the nineteenth century was now derided as anachronistic by the broader culture.

More confusing still was the fact that many evangelical women, like American women everywhere, had joined the workforce. On the one hand they were beset by calls for liberation and self-assertion from feminists, and on the other they were peppered from the pulpit by insistent rehearsals of the nineteenth-century ideal of femininity. Those who resisted the workplace inevitably felt anger and even shame about being labeled "just a housewife," and they protested loudly, if unconvincingly, about the nobility of tending the home.

Very often, economic necessity, an unemployed husband, or divorce tipped the balance in the general direction of the feminists. But many evangelical women were then left with what psychologist Leon Festinger calls cognitive dissonance: the contradiction between the necessity, on the one hand, of employment, and, on the other, the compunction they felt about not living up to evangelical standards. Many felt guilt and confusion for "abandoning" their homes and families, thereby violating the fundamentalist feminine ideal.

A question-and-answer exchange from the May 1989 issue of James Dobson's *Focus on the Family* magazine illustrates poignantly this confusion and anger, as well as a pining for a halcyon past. "As a homemaker," the question from an anonymous reader begins, "I resent the fact that my role as a wife and mother is no longer respected as it was in my mother's time. What forces have brought about this change in attitudes in the Western world?" Dobson's response is equally illuminating:

> Female sex-role identity has become a major target for change by those who wish to revolutionize the relationship between men and women. The women's movement and the media have been remarkably successful in altering the way females "see" themselves at home and in society. In the process, every element of the traditional concept of femininity has been discredited and scorned, especially those responsibilities associated with homemaking and motherhood.
>
> Thus, in a short period of time, the term housewife has become a pathetic symbol of exploitation, oppression, and – pardon the insult – stupidity, at least as viewed from the perspective of radical feminists. We can make no greater mistake as a nation than to continue this pervasive disrespect shown to women who have devoted their lives to the welfare of their families.[32]

Dobson, of course, failed to acknowledge that his "traditional concept of femininity" (presumably the one shared by his distraught reader) was a nineteenth-century construct. More significantly, Dobson's response identified the enemy: "radical feminists," the women's movement, and the media. In the face of such a conspiracy, evangelicals felt a need to muster their troops, something they did with remarkable success in the 1970s and 1980s, but in so doing they were forced to ignore, even to repudiate, the considerable support of evangelicals for women and women's issues in the nineteenth century.

What was especially striking about the exertion of evangelical influence in the American political arena at this point was the extent to which issues relating to gender – the proposed Equal Rights Amendment, the availability of abortion, private sexual morality – shaped their political agenda. Evangelicals, especially those associated with the Religious Right, regularly attached the adjective "antifamily" to policies and to politicians they regarded as inimical, and they have, curiously, paid singular attention to the issue of abortion.

In recent years, evangelicals have tried, with considerable success, to propel abortion to the center of political debate. A group of activists calling themselves Operation Rescue has picketed and blocked abortion clinics in New York, Atlanta, Wichita, Buffalo, and other cities around the country. Anti-abortion hecklers regularly disrupted Democratic Party rallies during the 1980s and 1990s.

The Supreme Court's 1973 decision in *Roe v. Wade*, which effectively struck down laws restricting a woman's right to an abortion, was initially greeted with silence or indifference by evangelicals – the Southern Baptist Convention actually endorsed the decision – but by the end of the decade, as conservative evangelicals began to mobilize, the abortion issue helped to galvanize them and make them a potent political force. Jerry Falwell, for instance, credited the *Roe v. Wade* decision with awakening him from his apolitical stupor, even though he had declared some years earlier that he "would find it impossible to stop preaching the pure saving gospel of Jesus Christ, and begin doing anything else – including fighting Communism, or participating in civil-rights reforms." "Nowhere are we commissioned to reform the externals," he had said then, articulating an attitude fairly common among evangelicals in the mid-1960s. "We are not told to wage war against bootleggers, liquor stores, gamblers, murderers, prostitutes, racketeers, prejudiced persons or institutions, or any other existing evil as such."[33] *Roe v. Wade*, however, together with what Falwell and others regarded as sundry other assaults on the family, triggered an about-face. By the end of the decade Falwell had organized his "Moral Majority" to counter the evil influences in American culture that threatened to subvert their way of life.

The very idea that a woman might seek an abortion violated the cherished evangelical ideal of feminine domesticity. If women guarded their purity and contented themselves with their divinely ordained roles as mothers and housewives, abortions would be unnecessary. For evangelicals, the very fact that abortion was a political issue in the first place provided an index of how dramatically American culture had deserted their ideal of femininity. The roots of the "disorder," then, could be found in female restiveness, an unwillingness to accept the role that God had designed for women. According to Susan Key, a homemaker from Dallas, Texas, who devised a course for women called "Eve Reborn," God gave women "a unique capacity for submission and obedience and when this capacity is thwarted by rebellion and deceit, it becomes a capacity to destroy which begins to work within her heart and then sulks out to her intimate relationships, widens to her acquaintances, to society, and then into history."[34]

But if benighted and wayward women contributed to this massive cultural malaise that evangelicals so decried, women also, because of their exalted spirituality, held the key to redemption. "I firmly believe the role of a woman today is to nurture our next generation," Maxine Sieleman of Concerned Women for America said during the 1988 presidential primaries, thereby echoing nineteenth-century evangelical notions of virtue. "She has the power within her hands to either make or break a nation. A good woman can make a bad man good, but a bad woman can make a good man bad. . . . Women are the real key for turning this country around. . . . I firmly believe that God has always worked through women."[35]

Phyllis Schlafly, who almost single-handedly defeated the proposed Equal Rights Amendment to the Constitution, said it more succinctly in *The Power of the Positive Woman*. The ideal woman, according to Schlafly, was not merely a housewife but a "patriot and defender of our Judeo-Christian civilization." Moreover, she added, "It is the task of the Positive Woman to keep America good."[36] Compare the sentiments of Catharine Beecher in *A Treatise on Domestic Economy*, published in 1841. "The mother writes the character of the future man; the sister bends the fibres that hereafter are the forest tree; the wife sways the heart, whose energies may turn for good or for evil the destinies of a nation," Beecher wrote. "Let the women of a country be made virtuous and intelligent, and the men will certainly be the same." Beecher added that "the formation of the moral and intellectual character of the young is committed mainly to the female hand."[37]

The agenda of politically conservative evangelicals late in the twentieth century, then, represented an attempt to reclaim the nineteenth-century ideal of femininity both for themselves and for a culture that had abandoned that ideal. For American evangelicals, women serve as a kind of cornerstone for the culture at large. If women allow themselves to be seduced by the "radical feminists" into abandoning their "God-given" responsibilities in the home, then America is in trouble. If, however, women enact the virtues of submission, nurture, and domesticity, then the future of the republic is secure. Far from being the temptress of earlier Christian orthodoxy, the contemporary woman, in the rhetoric of American evangelicalism, can be a redeemer. What better demonstration of her superior spirituality?

While evangelicals generally asserted the superiority of female piety, a 1990s movement of evangelical men, the Promise Keepers, drew on another vocabulary and tradition to celebrate — even to emulate — female piety in another way. Promise Keepers, the most recent incarnation of what has been called the "muscular Christianity" impulse in American history, traces its origins to an automobile trip between Boulder and Pueblo, Colorado. On March 20, 1990, Bill McCartney, then the head football coach at the University of Colorado, and his friend Dave Wardell were traveling to a meeting of the Fellowship of Christian Athletes, and in the course of their conversation they came upon the idea of filling Colorado's Folsom Stadium with men dedicated to the notion of Christian discipleship. This vision spread to a cohort of seventy-two men, who engaged in fasting and prayer in support of the notion.

Over four thousand men showed up for the first gathering, and by July 1993, McCartney's original vision had been fulfilled: fifty thousand men piled into Folsom Stadium for singing, hugging, and exhortations to be good and faithful husbands, fathers, and churchgoers. The organization, Promise Keepers, soon had an annual budget in excess of $100 million and offices in at least thirty-eight states. In 1996, perhaps the high point of the Promise Keepers' popularity, more than a million men attended twenty-two rallies at stadiums across the country.[38]

The venue was significant. Throughout church history, dating back to the New Testament, Christians have used athletic and military metaphors to describe spirituality. The apostle Paul admonished the early Christians to run the race, and to put on the full armor of God in their battle against the wiles of the devil. These themes have been played out in various ways across the centuries. Monks were spiritual athletes of a sort, training in godliness and implicitly competing with one another in the quest for holiness. The Crusades provided a religious legitimacy – and absolution – for military conquest, and the Society of Jesus was mobilized explicitly as the pope's army.

In American history, the military metaphor permeated nineteenth- and early- twentieth-century piety. It took various organizational forms – the Salvation Army, the Knights of Columbus, Awana Clubs, Christian Service Brigade, and Campus Crusade for Christ – but it also pervaded evangelical hymnody, as suggested by "Onward Christian Soldiers," "We're Marching to Zion," and "Rise Up, O Men of God."

Both the military and the athletic metaphors were especially appealing to men and were appropriated shamelessly in the muscular Christianity movement, which countered the notion that spirituality was a feminine domain and combined seduction and taunting in roughly equal parts. At the turn of the twentieth century, former professional athlete Billy Sunday cajoled the men in his audiences to "hit the sawdust trail" and give their lives to Jesus. "Many think a Christian has to be a sort of dishrag proposition, a wishy-washy, sissified sort of galoot that lets everybody make a doormat out of him," Sunday intoned. "Let me tell you the manliest man is the man who will acknowledge Jesus Christ."[39] A few years later, at about the same time that Charles Sheldon's novel *In His Steps* portrayed Jesus as an astute businessman, an organization called the Men and Religion Forward Movement summoned men back to the churches with the slogan "More Men for Religion, More Religion for Men." The campaign held rallies in places like Carnegie Hall, rented billboards on Times Square, and placed display ads in the sports sections of newspapers.[40]

Immediately after World War II, muscular Christianity drew more heavily on military metaphors, but the athletic ideal was never entirely absent. James C. Hefley published edifying biographical sketches of professional athletes who professed to be Christians: Bobby Richardson, Dave Wickersham, Bill Glass, Al Worthington, among many others. The movement encompassed such organizations as Athletes in Action (a subsidiary of Campus Crusade for Christ, thereby combining the motifs of militarism and athleticism), the Fellowship of Christian Athletes, and Power Team for Christ, a weight-lifting troupe which traveled to various venues and interspersed evangelistic testimonies with spectacular feats of strength.

By the late twentieth century athletics gradually eclipsed militarism as the predominant metaphor for evangelical spirituality. The Vietnam War had dimmed somewhat our collective enthusiasm for the military. Even Ralph Reed, formerly the executive director of Christian Coalition, claimed to eschew militaristic rhetoric. "Early in the 1990s, I occasionally used military metaphors for effect," he wrote in 1996. But Reed recognized the perils of such language and "sent out a memorandum to our grassroots leaders urging them to avoid military rhetoric and to use sports metaphors instead."[41] It should come as no surprise, then, that the Promise Keepers, embodying muscular Christianity in the 1990s, was suffused with an atmosphere of athleticism. McCartney, the founder, had led the University of Colorado Buffaloes from obscurity to national rankings and the Associated Press National Championship in 1990.[42] His rhetoric sometimes veered toward militarism – as when he declared, "We're in a war, men, whether we like it or not" – but Promise Keepers rallies and publications most often featured athletes, and each gathering took place in a sports arena.

The evangelical subculture – with its own language, imagery, institutions, and expectations – had pulled away from the American mainstream during the half century between the Scopes trial and Jimmy Carter's campaign for the presidency. It provided a place of refuge for beleaguered Protestants who felt alienated from the larger society and its values. Evangelicals, disturbed by the social and intellectual currents in the broader world, devised their own universe of congregations, denominations, Bible camps, Bible institutes, colleges, seminaries, publishing houses, and mission societies.

The evangelical subculture was marked by a fortress mentality, and in many ways it was a counterculture, in that it defined itself against the prevailing norms. It had its own rules and customs and standards. Whereas the broader culture was enamored of "modernist" ideas in science, theology, and culture, evangelicals stubbornly clung to traditional understandings of Protestant Christianity, upholding the virgin birth, the inerrancy of the Bible, and the authenticity of miracles.

One element of the larger culture especially did not sit well with evangelicals: feminism. It is no secret that, despite evangelicalism's noble heritage of activism on women's concerns in the nineteenth century,[43] feminist sensibilities have not flourished within twentieth-century American evangelicalism. The women's movement and the concomitant sexual revolution threatened evangelical mores, and evangelical leaders (an overwhelmingly male cohort) responded with determined attempts to reassert the ideals of feminine spirituality and domesticity.[44] Evangelicals blamed feminism for abortion, the rising divorce rate, the proliferation of sexually transmitted diseases, schoolchildren's low test scores, and a general moral decline in the country. A number of evangelical organizations were formed, notably Focus on the Family and Concerned Women for America, to counteract and to reverse the tide of feminism in the United States.

Here, on the issue of feminism – or, more precisely, in opposition to feminism – the world of sports and the evangelical subculture, as manifest in the Promise Keepers movement, intersected like circles on a Venn diagram, against a background of growing political discontent, especially within the white middle class. This so-called "white rage," which had been brewing for decades, fueled the political ambitions of Ross Perot in 1992 and has helped to sustain Pat Buchanan's endless campaign for the presidency. The contours of this discontent, rehearsed endlessly on talk radio – Liddy, Limbaugh, Michaelson, North – have been amply documented, but Thomas L. Friedman's column on the op-ed page of the New York *Times* during the 1996 presidential primaries provides a useful summary. "If the economy is doing so well, why have I just been downsized out of a job," Friedman asked rhetorically on behalf of his readers, "and why do I feel like my community is eroding?" Friedman and others have referred to this as the politics of resentment, and its symptoms include a belief that "our schools no longer teach right from wrong, that our nation can't control its borders and that patriotism is giving way to multiculturalism."[45]

The world, in short, is out of control. Order has given way to chaos.[46] This politics of resentment, when articulated by other oracles, has located different demons at different times. In the middle decades of the twentieth century these voices fingered Communism and the United Nations; later targets included the North American Free Trade Agreement (NAFTA), foreign aid, welfare, affirmative action, Hillary Rodham Clinton in particular, and feminism in general.

Feminism. Ever since the publication of *The Feminine Mystique*, women have not been content to stay at home, and, despite the well-publicized glass ceiling, they have entered every arena of American life, from the military to the Supreme Court, from the picket lines to the corporate boardroom. Every arena of American life save one: the sports arena. In spite of Title IX, sports are still segregated by gender, and the major organized team sports – those that culminate in the professional leagues that dominate the media and bring in the big money – constitute an all-male preserve. [47]

So the choice of venue for Promise Keepers rallies is revealing. In the first place, the world of athletics offers an orderly universe, a refuge from the larger world. What all major sports have in common since the age of industrialism are clear boundaries and precise delineations. The rules may be complex, but they are also precise, with every situation and contingency provided for. Something is either in bounds or out of bounds, safe or out, fair or foul. [48] Second, McCartney's affinity with football, as opposed to baseball or other sports, [49] underscores the sense of beleaguerment claimed by evangelical males. From its earliest origins in the bastions of privilege of the Northeast, football was unabashedly militaristic. One early enthusiast equated the brutality of warfare with the violence of football. "War," according to John Prentiss, Jr., a fullback, "is the greatest game on earth." [50] Whereas baseball, the game of immigrants engaged in an overwhelming struggle against stiff odds, represented a view of America from the bottom up, football, a game of brute force and relentless domination, offered an elite vision. The big three college football powerhouses at the turn of the century – Yale, Princeton, and Harvard – imposed their will on opponents, sometimes racking up scores in triple digits. [51]

If the domain of sports provides an alternative, orderly, male-dominated universe where the voices of women rarely intrude, the same could be said of Promise Keepers. Women were not allowed at Promise Keepers rallies because, the organization said rather vaguely, "the conferences are designed for specific men's issues in the context of an all-male setting." Women, they added, serve in a supportive capacity: "There are many women volunteers praying and working behind the scenes to ensure that these events go smoothly. One of the primary goals of the conference is to deepen the commitment of men to respect and honor women."

Indeed, the Promise Keepers campaign, which won a ringing endorsement from Beverly LaHaye, president of Concerned Women for America, had a great deal to say about men and their relationships with women. Promise Number Four (of seven) reads, "A Promise Keeper is committed to building strong marriages and families through love, protection and Biblical values." It would be difficult to gainsay the importance of such a sentiment, and part of the appeal of Promise Keepers was that it reassigned men to the private sphere in addition to the public sphere. But the ideology surrounding the campaign, with its paradoxical pairing of the soft-breasted male and a reassertion of patriarchalism, refused to acknowledge the corollary – that women could have a role in the workplace as well as the home. The essentialist ideal of femininity so desperately nurtured by the leaders of evangelicalism in the early twentieth century still demanded that women stay at home and remain submissive to their husbands.

In *Seven Promises of a Promise Keeper*, the 1994 manifesto of the movement, contributor Gary Smalley cites the case of the Brawner family, who live in a small town in Missouri. They have a son, described as "a national swimming champion and a freshman in college," a "17-year-old who's an outstanding three-sport athlete in high school," and Jill, "their beautiful and talented 13-year-old."[52] That description itself may be revealing: the sons are athletes – successful athletes – and the daughter is "beautiful and talented." Smalley goes on to describe the return of the eldest son from college and the potential for family tension because of an earring in one ear, part of his initiation to the college swim team. Mom, who is clearly a stay-at-home mother, meets him at the door, and after a brief exchange they wonder how Dad will greet this development when he returns from work. (After a moment of suspense, Dad, newly attuned to the demands of family life, manages to keep his temper.)

What, then, do evangelicals see as the role of men in the domestic sphere? After decrying "the feminization of the American male," which has "produced a nation of 'sissified' men who abdicate their role as spiritually pure leaders," Tony Evans, an African-American preacher who also served as chaplain to the Dallas Mavericks, made it clear that it is "proper — in fact, essential — for children to be nurtured, guided, and cared for by women." But men must, in Evans's words, reclaim their manhood and take charge of their households. "The first thing you do," he writes, "is sit down with your wife and say something like this: 'Honey, I've made a terrible mistake. I've given you my role. I gave up leading this family, and I forced you to take my place. Now I must reclaim that role.' " Evans insists that this is not a matter for negotiation. "Don't misunderstand what I'm saying here," he writes. "I'm not suggesting that you *ask* for your role back, I'm urging you to *take* it back." [53]

There can be little question that masculinity itself has been a protean notion in the latter half of the twentieth century. The Promise Keepers represent an intriguing response to that malleability, an impulse to impose order on a world widely perceived as chaotic, and to provide identity, direction, and solidarity for a cohort of white, evangelical, middle-class men. Much was made of the male bonding that took place at Promise Keepers rallies, but even that might be understood in the context of militarism and athleticism.

For the older, most senior generation of American males, military service in World War II and the Korean War often provided the venue for bonding with other men: strong ties of friendship and camaraderie were forged in bunkers, in air squadrons, or on board a destroyer. Many men of the next, the "baby boom" generation, come of age in the 1960s, had sought to avoid the draft, or they had returned embittered from Vietnam; they did not gather in VFW halls to swap war stories and renew ties with their war buddies. What bridged the gap between these groups of men and a third generation coming of age in the 1990s were stories of athletic prowess: the improbable touchdown pass, the no-hitter, Michael Jordan's latest violation of the law of gravity. Sports provides a common vocabulary for male interaction and bonding, so it was no accident that McCartney would choose sports arenas for his gatherings or that he would pepper them with sports personalities and athletic analogies. He was simply speaking the language of the disaffected male.

Many men felt confused and angry about the women's movement – shifting gender roles, changing sexual politics and expectations from the workplace to the bedroom. For many American males, feminism was disruptive. The responses were manifold, ranging from the primal yearnings of Robert Bly and *Iron John* to unabashed chauvinism and spousal abuse. But just as an interest in sports and sports memorabilia connotes a nostalgia for the simpler days of childhood and the quest for an orderly world, evangelicals' preachments about gender roles and so-called family values represent an effort to impose an order on what they perceive as the chaos created by feminism. What the world of sports and the evangelically inspired Promise Keepers movement had in common goes beyond the mere fixation with athleticism, where the criterion for superiority is usually physical strength and where men, therefore, can still dominate women. The Promise Keepers campaign, wittingly or not, tapped into a wider symbolic world that has resonated with American males. Both the athletic and the military metaphors point to dualistic views of the world; on the athletic field as on the battlefield, with rare exceptions there are winners and losers, and evangelicals' penchant for dualism in the twentieth century has been amply documented. [54] McCartney, drawing on male – specifically, *white* male – anxieties, marshaled the traditional Christian metaphors of militarism and athleticism to combat feminism, all behind the guise of a benevolent patriarchalism.

Both Promise Keepers and the world of sports provided the shelter of an orderly universe with its own standards, rules, and values. In a world perceived as disordered, both offer safety, a common language, shared assumptions, and the assurance of camaraderie.

We can only speculate how the political and cultural landscape of the late twentieth century might have been different had evangelical leaders chosen to build upon their historical legacy of activism on behalf of women and assumed their rightful place alongside leaders of the feminist movement. [55] Surely the presence of evangelicals would have tempered some of the more radical elements of the women's movement, but it is equally possible that the entire society might have arrived more quickly at something approaching a consensus in favor of equal rights and more flexible roles for all men and women. In such a scenario the Promise Keepers might very well have been superfluous.

CHAPTER SIX

Winning the Country Back

The Ironies of the Religious Right

It doesn't take much prompting for Duane Gish to launch into a jeremiad about America. Just like the Puritan preachers who decried the spiritual apathy they saw all around them in the seventeenth century, Gish, vice president for the Institute for Creation Research in Santee, California, believes that the signs of declension are obvious to even the most casual observer.

"Look at what's happening in this country in the last fifty years," he implores. "When I was a child I didn't know anybody who used drugs. I never even heard of such a thing. Today we have a rampant drug culture that is literally destroying the minds, the bodies, the very souls of millions of people." Gish is only warming to his topic. "We have an AIDS plague that is going to kill literally hundreds of millions of people here in the world. We have violence and crime on an unprecedented scale. We have teachers who are not even safe in their schools any longer." [1]

It is difficult to gainsay Gish's assessment – evidence abounds that ours is a society in turmoil – but American evangelicals disagree even among themselves about the reasons for the crisis they see enveloping the United States. Donald Wildmon, of the American Family Association, thinks that the responsibility for much of America's moral drift can be laid at the feet of television producers and programmers. Jerry Falwell and Pat Robertson blame, among other factors, the increased militancy of gays and lesbians. Randall Terry, of Operation Rescue, is certain that America's problems can be traced directly to the government's stubborn refusal to outlaw abortion, a circumstance that also, according to Terry, triggered the great flood in the Midwest in the summer of 1993 and ought to have disqualified Bill Clinton from taking the oath of office on a Bible.

Other conservatives have trained their sights on broader issues, especially those of gender, sexuality, and domesticity. James Dobson, of Focus on the Family, believes that America's malaise can be traced to the decline of traditional morality and so-called family values. Beverly LaHaye, head of Concerned Women for America, is one of many who believe that women have abdicated their responsibility for the spiritual welfare of their families and, by extension, the entire nation.

Duane Gish, as it happens, points to another source. The disorder and the chaos everywhere around us, he believes, can be traced to the fact that "judges, legislators, and educations, the leaders in our society" have been "indoctrinated and brainwashed" in evolutionary theory. "We know in our heart that there is a creator, a creator who created the universe," Gish continues. "I think that if we go back to that we'll have a much better society than we do today."[2]

For politically conservative evangelicals in America, the world of the late twentieth century is replete with dangers. The most striking characteristic of the demonology I have just described — evolution, abortion, homosexuality, television, the eclipse of "family values" — is its diversity. Thirty and forty years ago, most politically conservative American evangelicals could trace the world's ills to a single source — liberalism, or, more specifically, Communism (many evangelicals, especially the more militant fundamentalists, did not draw a distinction between the two). The scourge of Communism was responsible for unrest in the Third World, radioactive fallout, poor test scores among schoolchildren, the civil rights movement, and flouride in our drinking water. If only what Ronald Reagan would come to call the Evil Empire could be vanquished, then righteousness and Christianity and American probity — the three being virtually indistinguishable — could flourish.

The collapse of the Soviet Union rendered the world a more complicated place. Like it or not, it is human nature to define oneself in opposition to one's enemies, and for three-quarters of a century whatever else we knew about ourselves as Americans, we knew we were not Communists. The huge changes brought on by the demise of the Eastern bloc necessitated a radical rethinking of the world, and of America's place in what George Bush was the first to call the New World Order.

We see the paroxysms of those adjustments everywhere around us – in politics, in economics, and in diplomacy. But no group feels the burden of complexity more acutely than American evangelicals, who have long been accustomed to viewing the world in Manichean, dualistic terms – good *versus* evil, white *versus* black, freedom *versus* Communism.

The weakness for dualism – especially when combined with another ancient Christian heresy, Donatism, which insists on a separation from anything even remotely tainted by sin – has had many consequences for evangelicalism in the twentieth century. It lay behind the schisms that rent many Protestant denominations in the 1920s and 1930s, and it helps to explain the peculiar virulence with which evangelicals have dissented from the Federal and the National Council of Churches and the ecumenical movement generally. This in turn provides a key to evangelical rhetoric about "worldliness." Within the evangelical subculture, especially thirty and forty years ago, the most damning thing you could say about a fellow believer was that he was "worldly," that she had stepped over this dualistic divide and been seduced by the blandishments of the (outside) world.

Many evangelicals believe that women are especially susceptible to worldliness, and this is another reason why throughout much of the twentieth century they have imposed taboos on the wearing of jewelry and cosmetics, strict parietal rules that follow a woman until marriage, and, of course, severe restrictions on female sexual activity. Most also upheld the cult of true womanhood, which (as I, among many others, have argued) represented a response to the social changes that followed industrialization, the women's suffrage movement, and the advent of feminism.

At mid-century, fundamentalist firebrand John R. Rice lamented the rebellion of women against God-given and scripturally mandated authority structures, which made the woman subject to her father or her husband. Rice's book, *Bobbed Hair, Bossy Wives, and Women Preachers* (the title of which probably tells you as much as you need to know about the contents), explored the issue at length. "Bobbed hair is not so bad as bobbed character," Rice allowed. "The fashion of bobbed hair is forbidden because it is the symbol of the wicked fashion of rebellion of wives to their husbands' authority or of wicked daughters who rebel against their fathers."[3] Like any good Christian fundamentalist, Rice, moreover, believed that a renewed fidelity to the Bible would reverse the troubling tide of change. "Literally hundreds of women now have long hair as a result of hearing me teach and preach what God's Word says on that subject," he wrote. "Broken homes have been reunited as rebellious wives learned what God's Word has to say about a woman's submission to her husband and surrender to the will of God."[4]

The celebration of feminine nurture and domesticity, and the cult of true womanhood – which arose at a time of rapid urban growth and the emergence of an industrial, commercial economy – represent both a nostalgia for an idealized past and a fundamentalist longing for what they insist is a God-given and scripturally mandated social order. This reaction to modernity reached its apotheosis with the publication of Marabel Morgan's *The Total Woman* in 1973, exactly ten years after Betty Friedan published *The Feminine Mystique*. Even today, much of the anger that American evangelicals bring to the political arena can be traced to the resentments engendered by feminism and the sexual revolution, both of them direct challenges to evangelical certainties.

The advent of the "New World Order" presented evangelicals with new challenges. One continuous thread running through American foreign and domestic politics over the last several decades has been the sequential identification of external enemies. Many Americans fastened on the Japanese for a while, resenting their economic success on the grounds that it had come at our expense, perhaps even been purchased with postwar American dollars. The Arabs make good enemies, witness Desert Storm and the floodtides of nationalism it unleashed, but during that conflict there were, after all, good Arabs as well as bad Arabs, thereby skewing comfortable dualistic categories.

Bereft of a credible foreign enemy, Americans – led by spokesmen for the Religious Right – were forced to focus upon the enemy within. One might say that the collapse of the Soviet Union transformed the Cold War into a culture war.

One way to chart this transformation would be to compare the rhetoric of the Republican National Conventions of 1964 and 1992. In 1964, with the world deep in the throes of the Cold War, Barry Goldwater railed against Communism and admonished his audience that "extremism in the defense of liberty is no vice." At the 1992 convention, however, speaker after speaker warned of the perils *within* the United States. Patrick Buchanan was only too happy to enumerate them. At the top of his list was "radical feminism," followed by "abortion on demand, a litmus test for the Supreme Court, homosexual rights, discrimination against religious schools, women in combat units."[5] Pat Robertson made the transition from cold war to culture war explicit. "Seventy-five years ago a plague descended upon the world and covered the nations of Eastern Europe like a dark cloud," he began. "But, ladies and gentlemen, a more benign but equally insidious plague has fastened itself upon the families of America."[6]

For many Americans, our enemies, and hence our scapegoats, have become internal rather than external. Many evangelical leaders, especially the spokesmen for the Religious Right, have been busily identifying them: liberals, evolutionists, homosexuals, humanists, teenage mothers, "welfare queens," repeat offenders, abortionists.

Issues surrounding women and matters of gender still predominate. Women, because of their abandonment of so-called traditional roles, have been asked to bear much of the blame for America's supposed decline. The popularity of the term "femi-nazis," as propagated by radio talk-shows, provides an index of how widely gender prejudices are shared, as does the denigration of Hillary Rodham Clinton, who, despite her piety, has come to embody everything that politically conservative evangelicals fear: a woman who is intelligent, articulate, independent – in other words, out of control.

For American evangelicals there are many enemies among us, but none more pernicious than women who have heeded the siren call of feminism and turned their backs on the nineteenth-century cult of true womanhood, which once offered the refuge of an ordered domestic world. In the chaotic and disordered new world at the turn of the twenty-first century, American evangelicals still believe that women can bring at least a measure of order by hewing to so-called traditional roles, that therein lies the true power of femininity – the ability either to perpetuate chaos by insisting on female autonomy or to create order out of disorder through subordinating themselves to men. Small wonder that American evangelicals devote so much of their rhetoric to issues of gender and sexuality.

In the absence of a unifying vision, in the absence of comfortable dualisms, evangelicals have retreated again and again to the familiar redoubt of nostalgia. We're trying "to win the country back to the way it was," a fundamentalist pastor in Benicia, California, said, explaining his congregation's political activism within its community.[7] The role models for women offered by American fundamentalists – Sandi Patti, Marilyn Quayle, a white Christian gospel group called Point of Grace – evoke an earlier era. "If there's such a thing as an all-American person, that would be neat," exclaimed Terry Jones, a twenty-something member of Point of Grace, who makes a point of preaching virginity at the group's concerts. Then she amended her statement. "I don't know if I want to be called all-American the way America is today," she said. "Maybe all-American from the 50's or earlier."[8]

What about other elements of the Religious Right's agenda? Although its leaders periodically disclaim any intention of obliterating the distinction between church and state, their rhetoric and their actions suggest otherwise. Jerry Falwell, Pat Robertson, D. James Kennedy, and others are enamored of an ideology called Theonomy or Christian Reconstructionism, as articulated by Rousas John Rushdoony and by his estranged son-in-law, Gary North. Christian Reconstructionists believe that the civil government should conform to the Mosaic and Levitical laws of the Hebrew Bible. Capital punishment, for example, should be imposed for everything from sodomy to the incorrigibility of children. Reconstructionists especially detest the notion of toleration. North, one of the movement's most militant spokesmen, has insisted that "the perfect love of God necessarily involves the perfect hatred of God's enemies," and Rushdoony openly resents that "in the name of toleration, the believer is asked to associate on a common level of total acceptance with the atheist, the pervert, the criminal, and the adherents of other religions."[9]

While the more mainstream leaders of the Religious Right won't go quite that far – at least publicly – they have shown little sympathy for maintaining the wall of separation between church and state, religion and politics, established by the First Amendment. Their agenda includes all manner of attempts to collapse the distinction between church and state: mandating prayer in public schools, public support for religious education in the form of school vouchers, and the legal (not merely moral) prohibition against abortion under any circumstances.

Such stances, however, ignore the history of evangelical commitment to disestablishment and the separation of church and state. In particular, Robertson and Falwell, who claim to be Baptists, ought to know better: The noble tradition of church-state separation in America traces its roots to Roger Williams, who was also, not incidentally, the father of the Baptist tradition in America. Williams recognized the dangers of state interference in matters of faith, and Baptists joined with Thomas Jefferson and Enlightenment deists in insisting on disestablishment. Ever since – at least until the late 1970s – Baptists have been among America's staunchest defenders of disestablishment, in part because they were so adept at exploiting America's free market of religion.

Why have the leaders of the Religious Right, many of them Baptists, turned their backs on the principle of the separation of church and state? My only guess is that they no longer believe that they can compete in the free marketplace of religion in America. That is, they feel so overwhelmed by the successive waves of multiculturalism the United States has seen in the twentieth century that they seek some kind of advantage.

Although evangelicalism's standing as the most important social and religious movement in American history remains secure, the hegemonic hold that evangelicals once had upon the culture began to loosen late in the nineteenth century. Industrialization, urbanization, and the arrival of masses of non-Protestant immigrants, most of whom did not share evangelical scruples about temperance, began to dim evangelical expectations that the millennium, the one-thousand-year reign of righteousness predicted in the Book of Revelation, was underway. Teeming, squalid tenements infected with labor unrest on the Lower East Side of Manhattan and in other major cities bore no resemblance to the precincts of Zion so confidently predicted early in the nineteenth century. In addition, evangelicalism was buffeted by several intellectual challenges. The publication of Charles Darwin's *Origin of Species* in 1859, which sold out its first American printing in a single day, cast doubt on the Genesis account of creation, and, by extension, on one of the central tenets of evangelicalism, the literal truth of the Bible. Another alien notion, the German discipline of "higher criticism," further challenged the reliability of the Scriptures in general.

By the turn of the twentieth century, American evangelicals were reeling from these social, demographic, and intellectual assaults. They sought to shore up the ramparts of religious truth as they understood it. The publication of *The Fundamentals*, a series of pamphlets that appeared between 1910 and 1915, underscored their biblical literalism and announced their fidelity to conservative standards but cast them in a decidedly defensive posture. A decade later, the redoubtable and irascible H. L. Mencken, of the *Baltimore Sun*, heaped scorn upon evangelicals at the infamous Scopes "Monkey Trial" in Dayton, Tennessee, holding evangelicals and their beliefs up for public ridicule. Evangelicalism, especially its more militant strain, fundamentalism, became a byword for narrowness, bigotry, and anti-intellectualism, and evangelicals found themselves ostracized by the very culture they had shaped a century before.

For evangelicals in the early decades of the twentieth century, then, the trumpet call of triumphalism was drowned out by the rhetoric of retreat. Whereas evangelicals had so confidently predicted a righteous millennial kingdom a century before, they now wilted before the manifestations of a new kind of pluralism. They announced the imminent return of Jesus and gradually withdrew into their own subculture to await his arrival.

For half a century, roughly from 1925 to 1975, evangelicalism grew increasingly and intentionally separate from the larger culture, which its believers regarded as both corrupted and corrupting. During these decades evangelicals also undertook a truly remarkable building campaign; they formed their own congregations, denominations, mission societies, publishing houses, and a slew of Bible camps, Bible institutes, colleges, and seminaries. This evangelical retreat was a defensive move, and the subculture itself, this vast and interlocking network of institutions largely invisible to anyone but evangelicals, became a kind of fortress against the confusions of the larger world. They licked their wounds and convinced themselves that despite their overwhelming numbers they were a persecuted minority.

Evangelical frustrations finally surfaced in the mid-1970s, in the wake of Vietnam, Watergate, and the counterculture movement. The campaign and presidency of Jimmy Carter, a Southern Baptist, lured many evangelicals back into the larger political arena, but it is one of the many ironies of the Religious Right that, nationwide, politically conservative evangelicals abandoned Carter for Ronald Reagan in 1980. Responding to Reagan's promise to, in effect, enlarge the cocoon of the evangelical subculture to encompass, once again, the entire nation, they jumped on his bandwagon and enjoyed during his administration at least the illusion of power.

As evangelicals reentered the political arena, however, they soon learned that the rules of discourse had changed. The assumption that evangelical Protestants could set the terms of the debate, as they had been able to do in the nineteenth century, turned out to be sorely mistaken. Pluralism had brought other voices into the discussion, voices that did not share evangelical assumptions about sexual behavior, gender roles, biblical authority, or even about monotheism. For example, although evangelicals came late to the abortion question, they were surprised indeed that anyone would frame the issue in terms of legality and personal liberty rather than morality.

In response, the voices of the right-wing evangelical elite became more strident and indignant. In 1979, Jerry Falwell, pastor of the Thomas Road Baptist Church in Lynchburg, Virginia, set up an organization he called Moral Majority, warning that there was "no doubt that the sin of America is severe" and that the United States was "literally approaching the brink of national disaster." [10] Falwell and the Moral Majority sought to influence all dimensions of public policy. "I hope I live to see the day when, as in the early days of our country, we won't have any public schools," he declared in 1979. "The churches will have taken them over again and Christians will be running them. What a happy day that will be!" [11]

Other voices joined the fray. In 1980, Tim LaHaye, an evangelical pastor from El Cajon, California, published *The Battle for the Mind*, thereby signaling his entry into the arena of politics. The book, which was lauded by religious and political conservatives, was a full-throated assault on "secular humanism," which LaHaye found lurking behind such organizations as the National Organization for Women, the American Civil Liberties Union, the National Association for Education, and the United Nations. His wife, Beverly, mounted her own offensive by organizing a lobby of evangelical women, Concerned Women for America, that would, she argued, provide an alternative voice to feminism, specifically to that of the National Organization of Women. Beverly LaHaye conceded that she was "consumed" by the issue of homosexuality. "Of all the problems in America today," she said, "the homosexual movement poses the most serious threat to families and children."

The Religious Right found other oracles – James Dobson, Randall Terry, Gary Bauer, Lou Sheldon, Donald Wildmon – but none was more strident or vocal than Pat Robertson, who mounted his own campaign for the presidency in 1988. While attending the inaugural ceremonies for George Bush in January 1989, Robertson struck up a conversation with a young political operative, Ralph Reed, and the two collaborated in the formation of an evangelical lobbying organization called the Christian Coalition.

While Reed worked largely behind the scenes – organizing, building networks, and dispensing political advice – Robertson, using the platform of his own television network, supplied the rhetoric. He regularly excoriated Hollywood, feminists, homosexuals, abortion doctors, and political liberals – all of whom, he believed, were responsible for moral decay in the United States. When Disney World in Orlando, Florida, held "Gay Days" promotions, Robertson warned local residents to beware of "serious" hurricanes because the city had allowed homosexual groups to fly rainbow flags from light poles. "I don't think I would be waving those flags in God's face if I were you," Robertson declared, expanding his judgment to the entire nation. "A condition like this will bring about the destruction of your nation. It'll bring terrorist bombs; it'll bring earthquakes, tornadoes and possibly a meteor." [12]

Loss of hegemony can be frightening, and it can provoke a number of responses, from resignation to resentment and condemnation, from anger to action. Evangelicals have gone through all manner of contortions in an attempt to adjust to their changing status in American society. Having set the social and political agenda for much of the nineteenth century, evangelicals felt marginalized by cultural and intellectual currents of the late nineteenth and early twentieth centuries. Their initial response was withdrawal and even a sullenness, but a combativeness eventually reasserted itself. That combativeness has rested on two ideological foundations – an appeal to the so-called Judeo-Christian tradition and the idea of culture wars – both of which are highly suspect.

The leaders of the Religious Right in particular and neoconservatives in general frequently invoke the phrase "Judeo-Christian tradition." Usually this takes the form of a lamentation, a pining for the halcyon days before industrialization and social fragmentation ruptured American unity. But the best scholarship on the matter now suggests that the notion of a Judeo-Christian tradition was an artificial construct of the mid-twentieth century, an attempt beginning in the 1930s to close ranks against a new, ever widening pluralism in American culture. Will Herberg gave this construct the veneer of legitimacy in 1955, with the publication of his book *Protestant, Catholic, Jew.* Herberg enlarged the ambit of American respectability to include middle-class Jews and (non-Hispanic) Roman Catholics, but in so doing he effectively bracketed out all others.

Despite its questionable pedigree, the term "Judeo-Christian tradition" sounds compelling. But it presumes a kind of moral consensus between Christians and Jews that has never really existed, and the use of the term, repeated like a mantra by neoconservatives and the Religious Right, functions as a code for exclusion.

The second foundation for evangelical combativeness is the equally flawed culture wars construct. If Herberg lent credibility to the Judeo-Christian construct, James Davison Hunter did the same for the term "culture wars" in his book by that title, published in 1991.[13] In Hunter's world there are two opposing factions, the orthodox and the progressive (roughly, the conservative and the liberal), and he devotes several hundred pages to assigning voices to one side or the other. Some of the results are risible (like the insistence that former New York City mayor Edward I. Koch is a liberal), but the culture wars argument represents a wholesale flight from ambiguity and complexity in favor of a simplistic dichotomy. According to Hunter, these two sides, orthodox and progressive, are engaged in an all-out struggle for ascendancy, and the future of the nation will depend in large measure on which faction emerges victorious.

The culture wars typology is beguiling because it seems to provide a simple template for understanding the American social and political landscape. If we can just line everybody up on one side or another of the cultural divide, then we'll be able to make sense of the world. The culture wars construct has been appropriated by a Roman Catholic, Patrick Buchanan, most memorably at the Republican National Convention in 1992, but conservative evangelicals, who historically have demonstrated a weakness for dualism, have also picked up on it with a vengeance. Evangelical theology, with its stark contrasts between good and evil, sin and salvation, adapts all too easily to the bipolarity of such a framework.

The difficulty, however, is that while bipolarity may have worked during the fundamentalist-modernist controversy of the 1910s and 1920s, or during the Cold War, it no longer obtains in an ever more pluralistic context. The multicultural mosaic of American culture is far too diverse, the world is far too complicated to surrender to these simplistic categories. When Buchanan, who counted many politically conservative evangelicals among his supporters, thunders that in the "struggle for the soul of America, Clinton and Clinton are on the other side," it makes for a good sound bite and it stirs the passions of the Religious Right, but it grievously underestimates the realities of contemporary American society.

The ideological foundations may be flawed, but the electoral success of candidates marching beneath the banner of the Religious Right in recent years suggests that politically conservative evangelicals have touched a nerve. When Ronald Reagan intoned that America is and always has been a Christian nation, his remarks generated a warm response among those dissatisfied with the direction of American society in the latter decades of the twentieth century. The challenge of the counterculture, the ignominy of Vietnam, and the sting of Watergate all contributed to a sense that we Americans had lost our way. Carter called it a "malaise," but Reagan and the Religious Right seized on the opportunity to identify the enemies of America – both external and internal – as those responsible for the supposed decline in American righteousness.

In the best tradition of dualism, Reagan was unsparing in his attacks on the "Evil Empire" while evoking a powerful nostalgia for the simpler days of Ozzie-and-Harriet households (this despite the fact that Reagan himself was divorced and remarried). Again working from a dualistic typology, Reagan castigated liberals for America's domestic ills, everything from economic downturn to the breakdown of the nuclear family to low test scores in public schools.

This rhetoric, which was abetted by Falwell, Robertson, and others, built on real and widely shared fears and concerns. The rise in divorce rates since mid-century is indeed alarming; public education is in real trouble; we sometimes seem to have no moral consensus in America; and we are lacking in civility everywhere, from our expressways to grocery checkout lines to political campaign commercials.

If the symptoms are apparent, the solution is not. Neoconservatives and the Religious Right trot out the familiar bromides about returning to the foundations of the Judeo-Christian tradition. This, they insist, will undo the confusions of the twentieth century. All of our problems, they suggest, will dissipate if we outlaw abortion, institutionalize prayer in schools, and succumb to the chimera of a school voucher system.

Tragically, the voucher proposal, by allowing public money to be spent on private schooling, would undermine what has historically been our best tool for adaptation to pluralism and for countering social fragmentation. Known as common schools in the nineteenth century, public schools provided a meeting place where schoolchildren from different religions, ethnic backgrounds, and socioeconomic classes could meet to explore their differences – and their similarities – and forge friendships in the classroom or on the playing field. In the absence of homogeneity, public education remains our best chance for understanding one another.

Achieving moral consensus in a pluralistic culture is more elusive. How do we find an inclusive moral vocabulary that does no violence to any among our multitude of spiritual or religious traditions? Given the inherent exclusivity of the Judeo-Christian construct, the answer to this quandary is more difficult than it appears. The nonnegotiable premise underlying any serious discussion of this matter must be that the United States is a pluralistic society, but the larger question remains: How can we talk about morality without invoking religious categories that are exclusive? With such a herculean task ahead of us as we move into the twenty-first century, it is easy to understand why so many Americans are drawn to simplistic solutions.

The rhetoric emanating from the Religious Right – whether it be the language of culture wars or an evocation of the Judeo-Christian tradition – can be interpreted as a cry of frustration. Not everyone in this culture speaks the same language anymore – either figuratively or literally – as they (mostly) did in the nineteenth century. This helps to explain all the rhetoric about the United States as a "Christian" nation and about the need to return to so-called Judeo-Christian values.

The reentry of America's evangelicals into the arena of public life has been fraught with confusion and contortions; whereas in the nineteenth century, evangelicals, largely a united front, set the social and political agenda for the entire nation, when they returned to the arena of public discourse in the 1970s the social and political landscape had changed. They themselves no longer spoke with one voice – "social justice" evangelicals like Jim Wallis, Ron Sider, and Tony Campolo articulated new evangelical positions – and the leaders of the Religious Right discovered that they could not dominate the political agenda as their forebears had done in the previous century.

Sadly, in their reaction to the counterculture and to the perceived threats of liberalism and secular humanism, the leaders of the Religious Right, along with many politically conservative evangelicals, have betrayed the legacy of nineteenth-century evangelical activism, which was overwhelmingly concerned about the rights of women and the plight of the enslaved, the poor, and the destitute. In their zeal to institute prayer in public schools and to teach the Genesis account of creation as science, they have forgotten that religious sentiments have thrived in the United States like nowhere else in the West precisely because the exercise of religion has been voluntary, not coerced or compulsory.

The Religious Right has also changed its own rules of engagement. The so-called Reagan Revolution turned out to be a mirage; Ronald Reagan, who depended on the votes of politically conservative evangelicals, and who promised all manner of reforms, failed to prosecute their agenda as vigorously as they believed he would. Despite all the soaring rhetoric about America as the "shining city on a hill," the United States did not become evangelicalism writ large in the 1980s.

The activists of the Religious Right also discovered that the role of political insider had its limitations, so it was no accident that when Robertson and Reed formed the Christian Coalition in 1989 (the year after Robertson's abortive run for the presidency), they took up the rhetoric of marginality. To hear Robertson tell it – or Dobson or LaHaye or Sheldon or Wildmon – Christian conservatives are a persecuted minority perpetually under siege at the hands of Communists, Hollywood, liberals, homosexuals, feminists, and Hillary Rodham Clinton. In the face of the multicultural mélange of America in the late twentieth century, and a recent tendency some have decried as the "culture of victimization," the Religious Right has chosen to portray itself as an embattled minority despite its huge following.

"I want to be invisible," Ralph Reed once said of his political tactics. "I paint my face and travel by night. You don't know it's over until you're in a body bag. You don't know until election night." Guerrilla warfare doesn't adapt easily to discourse or negotiation. Having failed to dictate the terms of moral and political debate in the 1980s, those evangelicals who constitute the Religious Right have retreated once again, this time under the banner of an unfairly persecuted minority. They have done so in part, as the quotation from Reed indicates, to camouflage their machinations but also to appropriate the caché of minority status in a multicultural society. For evangelicals, this posture is disingenuous to be sure, but it is a strategy, they judge, that has worked for other groups in the latter decades of the twentieth century. Perhaps it will work for them as well.

The Vocabulary of Evangelicalism

The evolution of evangelicalism in America, where it became the most influential religious and social movement in U.S. history, has produced some rather specialized characteristics that set American evangelicalism apart from both its European roots and the mainstream of Protestantism in this country.

The visits of George Whitefield, an Anglican itinerant preacher, to the American colonies in the 1730s and 1740s triggered a widespread evangelical revival known as the Great Awakening. Despite the persistence of ethnic and theological differences, all manifestations of the Great Awakening emphasized the necessity of some kind of conversion followed by a piety that was warmhearted and experiential (or, in the argot of the day, "experimental") over against the coldly rationalistic religion characteristic of the upper classes and the ecclesiastical establishment. Although it is perilous to generalize about such a broad and internally diverse movement, evangelicalism in America has largely retained those characteristics: the centrality of conversion, sometimes known as the "born again" experience (the phrase is taken from John 3); the quest for an affective piety (perhaps best exemplified by John Wesley's Aldersgate experience in 1738, when he found his heart "strangely warmed"); and a suspicion of wealth, worldliness, and ecclesiastical pretension.

From the revival traditions of the eighteenth and nineteenth centuries to the militant fundamentalism of the 1920s to pentecostalism, with its emphasis on speaking in tongues and other gifts of the

Holy Spirit, evangelicalism is deeply imbedded in American life, in part because of its promises of salvation, intimacy with God, and membership in a community of fellow believers. It is a large and internally diverse movement which, according to polling data, includes anywhere from 25 to 46 percent of the population in the United States.

Fundamentalism

In the context of the religious history of the United States, the term "fundamentalism" refers to a subset of evangelicalism and is originally derived from a series of pamphlets called *The Fundamentals; or, Testimony to the Truth,* which appeared between 1910 and 1915. *The Fundamentals* contained conservative statements on doctrinal issues and were meant to counteract the perceived drift toward liberal theology within Protestantism. Those who subscribed to these doctrines became known as fundamentalists, and "fundamentalism" came to refer to the entire movement.

Fundamentalism has also been described as a form of antimodernism, but that characterization must be qualified. Fundamentalists are not opposed to modernism in the sense of being suspicious of innovation or technology; indeed, fundamentalists (and American evangelicals generally) have often been in the forefront in the uses of technology, especially communications technology. Fundamentalists have an aversion to modernity only when it is invested with a moral valence, when it represents a departure from orthodoxy or "traditional values," however these might be defined.

Finally, at least as it has developed in the United States, fundamentalism is characterized by a certain militancy; Jerry Falwell, for instance, has insisted that he is a fundamentalist, *not* an evangelical. This militancy – on matters of doctrine, ecclesiology, dress, personal behavior, or politics – has prompted George M. Marsden, the preeminent historian of fundamentalism, to remark that the difference between an evangelical and a fundamentalist is that a fundamentalist is an evangelical who is mad about something.

The Holiness Movement

Another of the strains of American evangelicalism is the holiness movement, which emerged from John Wesley's emphasis on Christian perfection, the doctrine that a believer could attain "perfect love" in this life, after the conversion or "born again" experience. Wesley's notion of perfect love freed the believer from previously accepted ideas about humankind's disposition to sin, although it allowed for failings rooted in "infirmity" and "ignorance."

Fittingly, holiness teachings achieved their best hearing in Methodist circles, but as Methodism expanded, became more respectable, and acquired middle-class trappings in the early nineteenth century, holiness doctrines faded into the background. Though rooted in the Methodist Episcopal church, the holiness movement was interdenominational and sought to revitalize piety in other denominations as well. Holiness – also called sanctification or second blessing (the first blessing is conversion) – theology was promoted in the antebellum period by Sarah Lankford and Phoebe Palmer in their "Tuesday Meetings for the Promotion of Holiness," by Timothy Merritt in his *Guide to Holiness* magazine, and by Charles Finney and Asa Mahan at Oberlin College. After the Civil War, the movement thrived in independent camp-meeting associations such as those at Ocean Grove, New Jersey, and Oak Bluffs, Massachusetts.

By the final decade of the nineteenth century, holiness evangelists numbered more than three hundred. The Methodist hierarchy grew uneasy about the movement's influence, however, especially the apparent lack of denominational loyalty among its participants. As they came under increased pressure, some of the movement's adherents submitted to the Methodist hierarchy, while others joined emerging holiness denominations such as the Church of God (Anderson, Indiana), the Church of the Nazarene, the Pentecostal Holiness Church, the Salvation Army, or the Fire-Baptized Holiness Church (among others). These groups generally emphasize the importance of probity and ask their adherents to shun worldliness in all its insipid forms. The holiness movement also survives in regular camp meetings throughout North America.

Pentecostalism

Pentecostalism coalesced as a movement in the early years of the twentieth century. On the first day of the new century – January 1, 1901 – Agnes Ozman, a student at Bethel Bible College in Topeka, Kansas, began speaking in tongues. This experience, also known as *glossolalia*, was explicitly linked to the first Pentecost, recorded in Acts 2, when the early Christians were filled with the Holy Spirit. The pentecostal movement, with its distinctive emphasis on the second blessing, or baptism of the Holy Spirit, spread quickly, first to Texas and then to Los Angeles (where it burst into broader consciousness during the Azusa Street Revival), and it took various denominational forms, including the Pentecostal Holiness Church, the Church of God in Christ, the Church of God (Cleveland, Tennessee), and the Assemblies of God, which was organized in 1914 and is the largest pentecostal denomination in North America.

Pentecostal worship today is characterized by a receptiveness to religious ecstasy embodied in the familiar posture of upraised arms, a gesture of openness to the Holy Spirit. Pentecostals generally believe in the gifts of the Holy Spirit, including divine healing as well as speaking in tongues.

The Charismatic Movement

The charismatic movement brought pentecostal fervor – including divine healing and speaking in tongues – into mainline denominations, beginning in the 1960s. Also known as the charismatic renewal or neo-pentecostalism, it erupted in 1960 among mainline Protestants with the news that Dennis J. Bennett, rector of St. Mark's Episcopal Church, Van Nuys, California, had received the baptism of the Holy Spirit and had spoken in tongues. About a hundred parishioners followed suit, much to the dismay of other parishioners, members of the vestry, and the Episcopal bishop of Los Angeles. Although Bennett left Van Nuys for Seattle, Washington, he remained with the Episcopal church, taking over a struggling parish, St. Luke's, and transforming it into an outpost of the charismatic movement.

Although the terms "pentecostal" and "charismatic" have come to be used almost interchangeably in recent years, Bennett's decision to remain an Episcopalian illustrates an important distinction: Whereas followers of both persuasions believe in the baptism of the Holy Spirit, pentecostals are affiliated with one of the pentecostal denominations (such as the Assemblies of God or the Church of God in Christ), while charismatics remain identified with traditions that, on the whole, look askance at pentecostal enthusiasm. Charismatic impulses, for instance, have also made their way into the Roman Catholic church, beginning in February 1967, when a group of faculty from Duquesne University in Pittsburgh attended a spiritual retreat and received the baptism of the Holy Spirit. The Duquesne Weekend, as it came to be known, led to other gatherings of Roman Catholics looking for spiritual renewal, notably in South Bend, Indiana, and Ann Arbor, Michigan, and the movement has spread well beyond those venues and into parishes throughout the country.

Notes

Introduction

1. Alexis de Tocqueville, *Democracy in America*, ed. Henry Steele Commager, trans. Henry Reeve (New York: Oxford University Press, 1947), 202.

2. Philip Schaff, *America: A Sketch of Its Political, Social, and Religious Character*, ed. Perry Miller (Cambridge, Mass.: Harvard University Press, 1961; original published 1855), 11.

3. G. K. Chesterton, *What I Saw in America* (London: Hodder and Stoughton, 1922), 12.

4. "Religion in America: 50 Years: 1935–1985," *The Gallup Report*, no. 236 (May 1985): 18, 50; ibid., no. 222 (March 1984): 28; Richard John Neuhaus, ed., *Unsecular America* (Grand Rapids, Mich.: Wm. B. Eerdmans, 1986), 119.

5. Theodorus Jacobus Frelinghuysen, *Sermons by Theodorus Jacobus Frelinghuysen*, trans. William Demarest (New York, 1856), 30–31.

6. Nathan O. Hatch, *The Democratization of American Christianity* (New Haven, Conn.: Yale University Press, 1989), 117.

7. Robert N. Bellah et al., *Habits of the Heart: Individualism and Commitment in American Life* (Berkeley and Los Angeles: University of California Press, 1985), 221.

8. Hatch, *Democratization*, 144.

Chapter One: CHALLENGING THE ROUTINE OF RELIGION

1. *Oxford English Dictionary*, 1971 ed., s.v. "Pietism."

2. See Martin H. Prozesky, "The Emergence of Dutch Pietism," *Journal of Ecclesiastical History* 28 (1977): 29–37; F. Ernest Stoeffler, *The Rise of Evangelical Pietism* (Leiden, Holland: E. J. Brill, 1971), especially pp. 109–79.

3. Henry Melchior Mählenberg, *The Journals of Henry Melchior Mählenberg*, 3 vols., trans. Theodore G. Tappert and John W. Doberstein (Philadelphia: Evangelical Lutheran Ministerium of Pennsylvania and Adjacent States, 1942–1953); Theodorus Jacobus Frelinghuysen, *Sermons by Theodorus Jacobus Frelinghuysen*, trans. William Demarest (New York: 1856).

4. A translation of Beissel's works appears in Peter C. Erb, ed., *Johann Conrad Beissel and the Ephrata Community: Mystical and Historical Texts* (Lewiston, N.Y.: Edwin Mellen Press, 1985); a manuscript of Freeman's "Mirror of Self-Knowledge" is at the New York Historical Society, New York City.

5. Randall Balmer, "John Henry Goetschius and 'The Unknown God': Eighteenth-Century Pietism in the Middle Colonies," *Pennsylvania Magazine of History and Biography* 113 (1989): 575–608.

6. Regarding Tollstadius, see Suzanne B. Geissler, "A Step on the Swedish Lutheran Road to Anglicanism," *Historical Magazine of the Protestant Episcopal Church* 54 (1985): 39–49; on van Dieren, see Douglas Jacobsen, "Johann Bernhard van Dieren: Protestant Preacher at Hackensack, New Jersey," *New Jersey History* 100 (1982): 15–29.

7. See, for example, Jon Butler, *The Huguenots in America: A Refugee People in New World Society* (Cambridge, Mass.: Harvard University Press, 1983); Ned C. Landsman, *Scotland and Its First American Colony, 1683–1765* (Princeton, N.J.: Princeton University Press, 1985), especially chap. 8; Randall Balmer, *A Perfect Babel of Confusion: Dutch Religion and English Culture in the Middle Colonies* (New York: Oxford University Press, 1989).

8. On Tennent's relationship with Frelinghuysen, see Milton J. Coalter, Jr., *Gilbert Tennent, Son of Thunder: A Case Study of Continental Pietism's Impact of the First Great Awakening in the Middle Colonies* (Westport, Conn.: Greenwood Press, 1986), especially chap. 1. Tennent's sermon, first preached at Nottingham, Pa., March 8, 1740, appeared in print as *The Danger of an Unconverted Ministry* (Philadelphia: 1740).

9. James Tanis, "Reformed Pietism in Colonial America," in F. Ernest Stoeffler, ed., *Continental Pietism in Early American Christianity* (Grand Rapids, Mich.: Wm. B. Eerdmans, 1976), 34–35.

10. Quoted in Edward T. Corwin, ed., *Ecclesiastical Records: State of New York*, 7 vols. (Albany, N.Y.: J. B. Lyon, 1901–1916), vol. 5, 3460.

11. Ibid., vol. 3, 2182–83.

12. See Erb, *Beissel and the Ephrata Community*; and *Ecclesiastical Records*, vol. 6, 3928.

13. *Ecclesiastical Records*, vol. 3, 1742.

14. Theodore G. Tappert, "The Influence of Pietism in Colonial American Lutheranism," in Stoeffler, *Continental Pietism*, 17.

15. See Prozesky, "Emergence of Dutch Pietism," 29–37; Stoeffler, *Rise of Evangelical Pietism*; F. Ernest Stoeffler, *German Pietism During the Eighteenth Century* (Leiden, Holland: E. J Brill, 1973).

16. See Randall Balmer, "The Social Roots of Dutch Pietism in the Middle Colonies," *Church History* 53 (1984): 187–99; Howard G. Hageman, "William Bertholf: Pioneer Dominie of New Jersey," *Reformed Review* 30 (1976): 73–80.

17. *Ecclesiastical Records*, vol. 2, 1349.

18. For an account of this schism, see Randall Balmer, "Schism on Long Island: The Dutch Reformed Church, Lord Cornbury, and the Politics of Anglicization," in William Pencak and Conrad Edick Wright, eds., *Authority and Resistance in Colonial New York* (New York: New York Historical Society, 1988), chap. 4.

19. Quoted in James Tanis, *Dutch Calvinist Pietism in the Middle Colonies: A Study in the Life and Theology of Theodorus Jacobus Frelinghuysen* (The Hague: Martinus Nijhoff, 1967), 54.

20. Joseph Anthony Loux, trans. and ed., *Boel's Complaint Against Frelinghuysen* (Renssalaer, N.Y.: Hamilton Printing Company, 1979), 53.

21. Balmer, "Goetschius and 'The Unknown God,'" 604; *Ecclesiastical Records*, vol. 4, 2896, 2881.

22. *Ecclesiastical Records*, vol. 5, 3493, 3541. (The word "coetus" is pronounced "SEE-tus.")

23. Ibid., 3533, 3499, 3649.

24. *Journals of Capt. John Montressor, 1757–1778*, New York Historical Society, *Collections*, Publication Fund Series 14 (New York: 1881), 350.

25. The word "subordination" became highly charged among the Dutch Pietists at mid-century; see, for example, *Ecclesiastical Records*, vol. 6, 3945, 3950, 4005, 4021.

26. A. G. Roeber has developed these ideas and posited a connection between legal and charitable concerns and the American Revolution in his "Ger-

mans, Property, and the First Great Awakening: Rehearsal for a Revolution?" in Winfried Herget and Karl Ortseifen, eds., *The Transit of Civilization from Europe to America: Essays in Honor of Hans Galinsky* (Tübingen, Germany: G. Narr, 1986), 165–84.

27. Richard M. Cameron, *The Rise of Methodism: A Source Book* (New York: Philosophical Library, 1954), 204.

28. See Nathan O. Hatch, *The Democratization of American Christianity* (New Haven, Conn.: Yale University Press, 1989).

29. See James D. Bratt, *Dutch Calvinism in Modern America: A History of a Conservative Subculture* (Grand Rapids, Mich.: Wm. B. Eerdmans, 1984); David Nyvall, *The Evangelical Covenant Church* (Chicago: Covenant Press, 1954); Arnold Theodore Olson, *The Search for Identity* (Minneapolis, Minn.: Free Church Press, 1980).

30. Quoted in Tanis, *Dutch Calvinistic Pietism*, 175.

31. Quoted ibid., 169; Balmer, "Goetschius and 'The Unknown God,'" 599.

32. Balmer, "Goetschius and 'The Unknown God,'" 591.

Chapter Two: DIVERSITY AND STABILITY

1. Alexis de Tocqueville, *Democracy in America*, ed. Henry Steele Commager, trans. Henry Reeve (New York: Oxford University Press, 1947), 200.

2. Robert Baird, *Religion in America*, abridged edition with an introduction by Henry Warner Bowden (New York: Harper & Row, 1970), 120, 110.

3. Philip Schaff, *America: A Sketch of Its Political, Social, and Religious Character*, ed. Perry Miller (Cambridge, Mass.: Harvard University Press, 1961; original published 1855), 11, 73.

4. Sidney E. Mead, *The Lively Experiment: The Shaping of Christianity in America* (New York: Harper & Row, 1963).

5. Winthrop S. Hudson, *The Great Tradition of the American Churches* (New York: Harper & Brothers, 1953).

6. See William G. McLoughlin, *New England Dissent, 1630–1833: The Baptists and the Separation of Church and State*, 2 vols. (Cambridge, Mass.: 1971); William G. McLoughlin, *Isaac Backus and the American Pietistic Tradition* (Boston: Little, Brown, 1967); John M. Mulder, "William Livingston: Propagandist Against Episcopacy," *Journal of Presbyterian History* 54 (1976): 83–104.

7. Perry Miller, *Roger Williams: His Contribution to the American Tradition* (Indianapolis, Ind.: Bobbs-Merrill, 1953), 98.

8. Ibid.

9. Jefferson's "Act for Establishing Religious Freedom" (1786), quoted in John F. Wilson and Donald Drakeman, eds., *Church and State in American History*, 2nd ed. (Boston: Beacon Press, 1987), 16.

10. Jefferson's letter to the Danbury Baptists, January 1, 1802, ibid., 79.

11. Quoted in Mead, *Lively Experiment*, 59.

12. Regarding the influences on the founders, see Garry Wills, *Inventing America: Jefferson's Declaration of Independence* (Garden City, N.Y.: Doubleday, 1978); James Tanis, "From Provinces and Colonies to Federated States: The Dutch-American Example," paper given at the Tenth Rensselaerswyck Seminar, Albany, N.Y., 19 September 1987.

13. T. H. Breen and Stephen Foster have argued that religious principles contributed to the stability of Puritan New England from settlement to the revocation of the charter. See their "The Puritans' Greatest Achievement: A Study of Social Cohesion in Seventeenth-Century Massachusetts," *Journal of American History* 60 (1973): 5–22.

14. From the charter granted by Charles II on July 8, 1663, quoted in Wilson and Drakeman, *Church and State*, 16.

15. Edward T. Corwin, ed., *Ecclesiastical Records: State of New York*, 7 vols. (Albany, N.Y.: J. B. Lyon, 1901–1916), vol. 5, 3460.

16. Quoted in Richard W. Pointer, *Protestant Pluralism and the New York Experience: A Study of Eighteenth-Century Religious Diversity* (Bloomington and Indianapolis, Ind.: Indiana University Press, 1988), 88.

17. In Wilson and Drakeman, *Church and State*, 95.

18. The most votes that a Communist Party candidate for president has received was just over 100,000 (out of more than 38,000,000) in the election of 1932; the Communist presidential candidate received 36,386 votes in 1984 (Marvine Howe, "U.S. Communists May Not Field a 1988 Slate," *New York Times*, 20 November 1987).

19. "No Excuse Not to Register," *New York Times*, 16 October 1987; Michael Oreskes, "An American Habit: Shunning the Ballot Box," ibid., 31 Jan 1988; "Voter Turnout Up Slightly, Reversing Trend," ibid., 8 November 1984; "Portrait of the Electorate," ibid., 10 November 1988. Religion, of course, also

serves as a conservative social force; for an excellent example of this, see Paul E. Johnson, *A Shopkeeper's Millennium: Society and Revivals in Rochester, New York, 1815–1837* (New York: Hill and Wang, 1978). See also Joseph R. Gusfield, *Symbolic Crusade: Status Politics and the American Temperance Movement* (Urbana, Ill.: University of Illinois Press, 1963); Charles C. Cole, Jr., *The Social Ideas of the Northern Evangelists, 1826–1860* (New York: Columbia University Press, 1954).

20. Religious groups have a vested interest in upholding the claims of the state because of the tax exemptions granted to religious organizations by all levels of government.

21. De Tocqueville, *Democracy in America*, 200.

22. *Washington's "Farewell Address" in Facsimile, with Transliterations of All the Drafts of Washington, Madison, and Hamilton, Together with their Correspondence and Other Supporting Documents*, ed. Victor Hugo Paltsits (New York: New York Public Library, 1935), 151.

23. I express some hesitation about the quotation because it has never been documented that Eisenhower actually said it, although it is frequently attributed to him; see Patrick Henry, "'And I Don't Care What It Is': The Tradition-History of a Civil-Religion Proof Text," *Journal of the American Academy of Religion* 49 (1981): 35–49.

24. Breen and Foster argue that the general prosperity of seventeenth-century New England contributed to its stability ("The Puritans' Greatest Achievement").

25. Schaff, *America*, 79.

26. Ibid., 78.

27. De Tocqueville, *Democracy in America*, 202.

28. "Religion in America: 50 Years: 1935–1985," *The Gallup Report*, no. 236 (May 1985): 18, 50; ibid., no. 222 (March 1984): 28; Richard John Neuhaus, ed., *Unsecular America* (Grand Rapids, Mich.: W. B. Eerdmans, 1986), 119.

29. Philip Norman, *Shout! The Beatles in Their Generation* (New York: Simon & Schuster, 1981), 265–66.

30. Francis X. Clines, "With Bare Churches, It's Barely England's Church," *New York Times*, 11 May 1987.

31. On American latitudinarianism in religion, see Patricia U. Bonomi, *Under the Cope of Heaven: Religion, Society, and Politics in Colonial America* (New

York: Oxford University Press, 1986), 218–20; Robert N. Bellah et al., *Habits of the Heart: Individualism and Commitment in American Life* (Berkeley and Los Angeles: University of California Press, 1985), chap. 9.

32. Quoted in Edwin S. Gaustad, *Liberty of Conscience: Roger Williams in America* (Grand Rapids, Mich.: Wm. B. Eerdmans, 1991), 167.

33. Quoted ibid., 189.

Chapter Three: VISIONS OF RAPTURE

1. See Alan Rogerson, *Millions Now Living Will Never Die: A Study of Jehovah's Witnesses* (London: Constable, 1969); Albert V. Vandenberg, "Charles Taze Russell: Pittsburgh Prophet, 1879–1909," *Western Pennsylvania Historical Magazine* 69 (January 1986): 3–20; Edwin Scott Gaustad, *Dissent in American Religion* (Chicago: University of Chicago Press, 1973), 114–16. On the Good Friday vigil, see Barbara Grizzuti Harrison, *Visions of Glory: A History and a Memory of Jehovah's Witnesses* (New York: Simon & Schuster, 1978), 51; Rogerson, *Millions Now Living*, 9.

2. *Signs of the Times*, 15 April 1840, p. 14. Biographical details from Everett N. Dick, "The Millerite Movement, 1830–1845," in Gary Land, ed., *Adventism in America* (Grand Rapids, Mich.: Wm. B. Eerdmans, 1986).

3. Dick, "Millerite Movement," 9, 13–15.

4. Ibid., 18.

5. Ibid., 29–30; on the "ascension robes," see 21–22.

6. Regarding this rather tortuous transition, see Jonathan Butler, "From Millerism to Seventh-Day Adventism: 'Boundlessness to Consolidation,'" *Church History* 55 (1986): 50–64. On Seventh-Day Adventist membership statistics, see Land, *Adventism in America*, appendix 2.

7. See Pauline Moffitt Watts, "Prophecy and Discovery: On the Spiritual Origins of Christopher Columbus's 'Enterprise of the Indies,'" *American Historical Review* 90 (1985): 73–102. Moffitt argues that although the historiography (especially Samuel Eliot Morison's *The Admiral of the Ocean Sea*) has portrayed Columbus as a man of science and rationality, Columbus was increasingly consumed by apocalyptic ideology and his own destiny.

8. Carl Whorley, who describes himself as pastor/teacher at the Tanglewood Baptist Church, Roanoke, Va., offers a fairly standard evangelical definition for the Rapture: a "special event when the Lord Jesus Christ Himself will come

down from heaven and hover over the earth. He will call the dead, born-again Christians out of the grave, and then after that the saints who are alive and still on this earth at this event. He will then take them off of the earth as well and take them back to heaven to be with Him" (transcript of cassette tape entitled "The Rapture of the Church," distributed by Tanglewood Baptist Church, Roanoke, Va.).

9. For a survey of various views, see Robert G. Clouse, ed., *The Meaning of the Millennium: Four Views* (Downers Grove, Ill.: InterVarsity Press, 1977). Timothy P. Weber has diagrammed some of the various possibilities; see *Living in the Shadow of the Second Coming: American Premillennialism 1875–1982*, 2d ed. (Grand Rapids, Mich.: Zondervan, 1983), 10.

10. For Edwards's apocalyptic views, see *The Works of Jonathan Edwards*, vol. 5: *Apocalyptic Writings*, ed. Stephen J. Stein (New Haven, Conn.: Yale University Press, 1977), 27–29.

11. Quoted in Robert S. Fogarty, ed., *American Utopianism* (Itasca, Ill.: F. E. Peacock, 1972), 18. For an explication of complex marriage and its millennial justification, see Constance Noyes Robertson, *Oneida Community: An Autobiography, 1851–1876* (Syracuse, N.Y.: Syracuse University Press, 1970), chap. 9.

12. Nathan O. Hatch, *The Sacred Cause of Liberty: Republican Thought and the Millennium in Revolutionary New England* (New Haven, Conn.: Yale University Press, 1977); Ruth Bloch, *Visionary Republic: Millennial Themes in American Thought, 1756–1800* (Cambridge: Cambridge University Press, 1985), chaps. 2–4. On the connection between New Light evangelicalism and Patriotism, see also Alan Heimert, *Religion and the American Mind from the Great Awakening to the Revolution* (Cambridge, Mass.: Harvard University Press, 1966). Melvin B. Endy, Jr., takes issue with interpretations of the American Revolution that posit strong undercurrents of millennialism in the Patriot rhetoric. Endy insists that evangelicals more often cast their rationalizations for Revolution in the language of just war theory. See "Just War, Holy War, and Millennialism in Revolutionary America," *William and Mary Quarterly*, 3d ser., 42 (1985): 3–25.

13. Quoted in Peter N. Moore, "Westward the Course of Empire: Hermon Husband and the Frontier Millennium," typescript of a paper lent by the author. On Husband, see also Bloch, *Visionary Republic*, 72–74, 113–14, 182–84.

14. This latter point is made by Douglas Frank, *Less Than Conquerors: How*

Evangelicals Entered the Twentieth Century (Grand Rapids, Mich.: Wm. B. Eerdmans, 1986), 67. Nathan O. Hatch touches on this as well in "Millennialism and Popular Religion in the Early Republic," in Leonard I. Sweet, ed., *The Evangelical Tradition in America* (Macon, Ga.: Mercer University Press, 1984), 113–30.

15. On millennial themes in early American history, see James West Davidson, *The Logic of Millennial Thought: Eighteenth-Century New England* (New Haven, Conn.: Yale University Press, 1977); Hatch, *Sacred Cause of Liberty*; Bloch, *Visionary Republic*; James H. Moorhead, "Between Progress and Apocalypse: A Reassessment of Millennialism in American Religious Thought, 1800–1880," *Journal of American History* 71 (1984): 524–42; Ernest Lee Tuveson, *Redeemer Nation: The Idea of America's Millennial Role* (Chicago: University of Chicago Press, 1968). Regarding the various social reform movements arising out of the Second Great Awakening, see Timothy L. Smith, *Revivalism and Social Reform in Mid-Nineteenth-Century America* (Nashville, Tenn.: Abingdon Press, 1967); Charles I. Foster, *An Errand of Mercy: The Evangelical United Front, 1790–1837* (Chapel Hill, N.C.: University of North Carolina Press, 1960); Anne M. Boylan, "Women in Groups: An Analysis of Women's Benevolent Organizations in New York and Boston, 1797–1840," *Journal of American History* 71 (1984): 497–523.

16. William G. McLoughlin says that the message of this song is "one of millennial faith and optimistic conviction that God has chosen the *United States* of America to lead the way to the redemption of the world for Christian freedom" (William G. McLoughlin, ed., *The American Evangelicals, 1800–1900: An Anthology* [New York: Harper & Row, 1968], 28; "The Battle Hymn of the Republic" is reproduced on 28–29).

17. Quoted in James H. Moorhead, *American Apocalypse: Yankee Protestants and the Civil War, 1860–1869* (New Haven, Conn.: Yale University Press, 1978), ix. Moorhead's book is an excellent, extended study of the millennial views of northern Protestants during the Civil War.

18. William Robbins, "Mormons Go Back to a Sacred Valley in Missouri," *New York Times*, 14 August 1985. On Mormon millennialism, see Klaus Hansen, *Quest for Empire: The Political Kingdom of God and the Council of Fifty* (East Lansing, Mich.: Michigan State University Press, 1967); Grant Underwood,

"Early Mormon Millenarianism: Another Look," *Church History* 54 (1985): 215–29.

19. Quoted in Eric Foner, ed., *Great Lives Observed: Nat Turner* (Englewood Cliffs, N.J.: Prentice-Hall, 1971), 45.

20. Quoted in Milton C. Sernett, ed., *Afro-American Religious History: A Documentary Witness* (Durham, N.C.: Duke University Press, 1985), 95.

21. On the eclipse of postmillennialism in the late nineteenth century, see Weber, *Living in the Shadow*, chap. 2; James H. Moorehead, "The Erosion of Postmillennialism in American Religious Thought, 1865–1925," *Church History* 53 (1984): 61–77. Moorehead argues that postmillennialism collapsed, in effect, beneath its own weight, that it could be sustained only in a culture dominated by evangelical values.

22. For a discussion of Darby's views and their implications, see Weber, *Living in the Shadow*, chap. 1.

23. On the transition from postmillennialism to premillennialism and its importance to American evangelicals, see George M. Marsden, *Fundamentalism and American Culture: The Shaping of Twentieth-Century Evangelicalism, 1870–1925* (Grand Rapids, Mich.: Wm. B. Eerdmans, 1980), 48–55; Moorehead, "Erosion of Postmillennialism"; Frank, *Less Than Conquerors*, chap. 3. Frank sees the evangelical shift to premillennialism as an attempt to "recapture their control of history" (ibid., 67). On the influence of British millennial ideas in nineteenth-century America, see Ernest R. Sandeen, *The Roots of Fundamentalism: British and American Millenarianism, 1800–1930* (Chicago: University of Chicago Press, 1970).

24. Quoted in McLoughlin, *American Evangelicals*, 184.

25. Grant Wacker, "Marching to Zion: Religion in a Modern Utopian Community," *Church History* 54 (1985): 496–511.

26. Quoted in Weber, *Living in the Shadow*, 88.

27. The Scofield Reference Bible remains popular. Oxford, according to Cynthia Read, religion editor, has sold well over 2 million copies since 1967, 85% of them leather-bound (an indication that the overwhelming majority of copies sold are for personal, devotional use, rather than for use in libraries).

28. Evangelicals see the creation of the state of Israel in 1948 as the fulfillment of the prophecy found in Jeremiah 29:14: "I will be found by you, says the

Lord, and I will restore your fortunes and gather you from all the nations and all the places where I have driven you, says the Lord, and I will bring you back to the place from which I sent you into exile" (RSV).

29. Quoted in William Martin, "Waiting for the End: The Growing Interest in Apocalyptic Prophecy," *Atlantic Monthly*, June 1982, 35; cf. George Marsden, "Lord of the Interior," *Reformed Journal* 31 (June 1981): 2–3.

30. Evangelical hymns are replete with references to the coming millennium. Fanny Crosby's hymn, "Will Jesus Find Us Watching?" provides one example:

> When Jesus comes to reward His servants,
> Whether it be noon or night,
> Faithful to Him will He find us watching
> With our lamps all trimmed and bright?
>
> Blessed are those whom the Lord finds watching,
> In His glory they shall share;
> If He shall come at dawn or midnight,
> Will He find us watching there?

(Quoted in Weber, *Living in the Shadow*, 60.) Another, more recent song, written by Andraé Crouch, reads in part:

> It won't be long till we'll be leaving here.
> It won't be long. We'll be going home.

31. Martin, "Waiting for the End," 31.

32. As in the nineteenth century, twentieth-century African-American visions of the apocalypse take a slightly different form. The Honorable Elijah Muhammad taught that after six thousand years of white dominance, the "spook civilization" would come to an end about the year 2000. For the most compelling exposition of these ideas, see Malcolm X, *The Autobiography of Malcolm X* (New York: Grove Press, 1964), chaps. 10–11.

1. Harry S. Stout, "Religion, Communications, and the Ideological Origins of the American Revolution," *William and Mary Quarterly*, 3d ser., 34 (1977): 519–41.

2. Alexis de Tocqueville, *Democracy in America*, ed. Henry Steele Commager, trans. Harry Reeve (New York: Oxford University Press, 1947), 102.

3. Daniel Walker Howe, "Religion and Politics in the Antebellum North," in Mark A. Noll, ed., *Religion and American Politics: From the Colonial Period to the 1980s* (New York: Oxford University Press, 1990), 124–25.

4. See Rhys Isaac, *The Transformation of Virginia, 1740–1790* (Chapel Hill, N.C.: University of North Carolina Press, 1982), 267–69.

5. Quoted in Robert W. Cherny, *A Righteous Cause: The Life of William Jennings Bryan* (Boston: Little, Brown, 1985), 58.

6. Peter Cartwright, *The Autobiography of Peter Cartwright* (Nashville, Tenn.: Abingdon Press, 1956), 43.

7. Quoted in William Martin, *A Prophet with Honor: The Billy Graham Story* (New York: 1991), 111.

8. Philip Schaff, *America: A Sketch of Its Political, Social, and Religious Character*, ed. Perry Miller (Cambridge, Mass.: Harvard University Press, 1961; original published 1855), 95.

9. Quoted in James Tanis, *Dutch Calvinistic Pietism in the Middle Colonies: A Study in the Life and Theology of Theodorus Jacobus Frelinghuysen* (The Hague: Martinus Nijhoff, 1967), 54.

10. Quoted in Randall Balmer, *A Perfect Babel of Confusion: Dutch Religion and English Culture in the Middle Colonies* (New York: Oxford University Press, 1989), 127, 125.

11. Quoted in Leigh Eric Schmidt, "'A Second and Glorious Reformation': The New Light Extremism of Andrew Croswell," *William and Mary Quarterly*, 3d ser., 43 (1986): 222.

12. Harry S. Stout and Peter Onuf, "James Davenport and the Great Awakening in New London," *Journal of American History* 70 (1983): 556–78.

13. Isaac, *Transformation of Virginia*.

14. Richard L. Bushman, ed., *The Great Awakening: Documents on the Revival of Religion, 1740–1745* (New York: Atheneum, 1970), 50, 57.

15. John F. Wilson and Donald Drakeman, eds., *Church and State in American History*, 2d ed. (Boston: Beacon Press, 1987), 59.

16. Richard Allen, *The Life Experience and Gospel Labors of the Rt. Rev. Richard Allen* (Nashville, Tenn.: Abingdon Press, 1983), 30.

17. Quoted in Nathan O. Hatch, *The Democratization of American Christianity* (New Haven, Conn.: Yale University Press, 1989), 20.

18. Cartwright, *Autobiography*, 61.

19. Betty I. Young, "A Missionary/Preacher as America Moved West: The Ministry of John Wesley Osborne," *Methodist History* 24 (1986): 195–215.

20. *The American Colporteur System* (New York: American Tract Society, 1836), 3; reprinted in *The American Tract Society Documents, 1824–1925* (New York: Arno Press, 1972).

21. Ibid., 7.

22. Ibid., 9.

23. Young, "Missionary/Preacher," 208–9.

24. *Instructions of the Executive Committee of the American Tract Society, to Colporteurs and Agents, with Statements of the History, Character, and Object of the Society* (New York: 1868), 47; reprinted in *American Tract Society Documents*.

25. Ibid., 38–39.

26. Douglas Frank, *Less than Conquerors: How Evangelicals Entered the Twentieth Century* (Grand Rapids, Mich.: Wm. B. Eerdmans, 1986), 173–79.

27. See Edith L. Blumhofer, *Aimee Semple McPherson: Everybody's Sister* (Grand Rapids, Mich.: Wm. B. Eerdmans, 1993); William G. McLoughlin, "Aimee Semple McPherson: 'Your Sister in the King's Glad Service,'" *Journal of Popular Culture* 1 (1967): 193–217.

28. Quoted in Cherny, *Righteous Cause*, 60.

29. Quoted ibid., 34.

Chapter Five: A LOFTIER POSITION

1. Robert J. Samuelson, "Great Expectations," *Newsweek*, 8 January 1996, 27.

2. Bailey Smith on *Larry King Live*, 21 March 1989.

3. Edward M. Brandt, "Mother," *The Way of Truth*, May 1989, 2.

4. Barbara A. Peil, "A Seasoned Approach," *Kindred Spirit* 11 (Spring 1987): 13.

5. Nancy Tucker, "Motherhood in the '90s," *Focus on the Family* 14 (January 1990): 2.

6. Brandt, "Mother," ii, 1.

7. Peil, "Seasoned Approach," 12.

8. Ibid., 13.

9. This argument is made forcefully and compellingly by R. Marie Griffith in *God's Daughters: Evangelical Women and the Power of Submission* (Berkeley and Los Angeles: University of California Press, 1997).

10. Peil, "Seasoned Approach," 12.

11. Rosemary Radford Ruether and Rosemary Skinner Keller, eds., *Women and Religion in America*, 3 vols. (San Francisco: Harper & Row, 1981–1986), vol. 2, 161.

12. Gerald F. Moran, "'Sisters in Christ': Women and the Church in Seventeenth-Century New England," in Janet Wilson James, ed., *Women in American Religion* (Philadelphia: University of Pennsylvania, 1976), 47–65; Laurel Thatcher Ulrich, "Vertuous Women Found: New England Ministerial Literature, 1668–1735," ibid., 67–88.

13. Ruth H. Bloch, "The Gendered Meanings of Virtue in Revolutionary America," *Signs* 13 (1987): 37–58.

14. See Jan Lewis, "The Republican Wife: Virtue and Seduction in the Early Republic," *William and Mary Quarterly*, 3d ser., 44 (1987): 689–721.

15. Susan Juster writes, "The restoration of agency is the key to understanding women's experience of grace. . . . These women were empowered by recovering their sense of self through the assertion of independence from others," in "'In a Different Voice': Male and Female Narratives of Religious Conversion in Post-Revolutionary America," *American Quarterly* 41 (1989): 53.

16. Ruether and Keller, *Women and Religion in America*, vol. 1, 34.

17. Ibid., vol. 2, 402.

18. Ibid., vol. 1, 36.

19. Catharine E. Beecher and Harriet Beecher Stowe, *The American Woman's Home; or, Principles of Domestic Science; being a Guide to the Formation*

and Maintenance of Economical Healthful Beautiful and Christian Homes (New York: 1869), 19.

20. Alexis de Tocqueville, *Democracy in America*, ed. Henry Steele Commager, trans. Henry Reeve (New York: Oxford University Press, 1947), 401, 403.

21. Ann Douglas, *The Feminization of American Culture* (New York: Anchor Books, 1977).

22. Mary P. Ryan, "A Women's Awakening: Evangelical Religion and the Families of Utica, New York, 1800–1840," in James, *Women in American Religion*, 107.

23. *Women and Religion in America*, vol. 2, 401.

24. Sylvester Graham, *A Treatise on Bread, and Bread-Making* (Boston: 1837), 105–6.

25. Catharine E. Beecher, *A Treatise on Domestic Economy, for the Use of Young Ladies at Home, and at School* (Boston: 1841), 9.

26. These ideas of Victorian domestic culture are developed nicely by Colleen McDannell, *The Christian Home in Victorian America, 1840–1900* (Bloomington and Indianapolis, Ind.: Indiana University Press, 1986).

27. The "feminization" of American Protestantism in the nineteenth century extended well beyond the evangelical ambit, and so did the various reclamation efforts early in the twentieth. See Gail Bederman, " 'The Women Have Had Charge of the Church Work Long Enough': The Men and Religion Forward Movement of 1911–1912 and the Masculinization of Middle-Class Protestantism," *American Quarterly* 61 (1989): 432–65.

28. Quoted in Douglas Frank, *Less than Conquerors: How Evangelicals Entered the Twentieth Century* (Grand Rapids, Mich.: Wm. B. Eerdmans, 1986), 192.

29. *Women and Religion in America*, vol. 3, 260, 261.

30. Ibid., 261, 262.

31. Marabel Morgan, *The Total Woman* (Old Tappan, N.J.: Fleming H. Revell, 1973), 55.

32. "Dr. Dobson Answers Your Questions," *Focus on the Family* 13 (May 1989): 8.

33. Quoted in Frances FitzGerald, "A Disciplined, Charging Army," *New Yorker*, 18 May 1981, 63.

34. Quoted in Carol Flake, *Redemptorama: Culture, Politics, and the New Evangelicalism* (Garden City, N.Y.: Anchor Press, 1984), 70.

35. Quoted in Randall Balmer, *Mine Eyes Have Seen the Glory: A Journey into the Evangelical Subculture in America* (New York: Oxford University Press, 1989), 120–21.

36. Quoted in Flake, *Redemptorama*, 87.

37. Beecher, *Treatise on Domestic Economy*, 13.

38. "Religious Extremism, Religious Truth," *Christian Century*, 20–27 December 1995, 1236.

39. Quoted in Frank, *Less than Conquerors*, 193.

40. See Bederman, "'The Women Have Had Charge,'" 432–65.

41. Ralph Reed, *Active Faith: How Christians Are Changing the Soul of American Politics* (New York: Free Press, 1996), 120.

42. McCartney retired after the 1994 season "to spend time with his family and to pursue a closer personal relationship with God."

43. On the tradition of evangelical activism, which derives primarily from the holiness-pentecostal wing of evangelicalism, see Donald W. Dayton, *Discovering an Evangelical Heritage* (Peabody, Mass.: Hendrickson, 1976), especially chap. 8.

44. See Betty A. DeBerg, *Ungodly Women: Gender and the First Wave of American Fundamentalism* (Minneapolis, Minn.: Fortress Press, 1990).

45. Thomas L. Friedman, "Buchanan for President," *New York Times*, 24 December 1995, 9.

46. Margaret Lamberts Bendroth argues that much of the appeal of dispensational premillennialism (and its concomitant success in defining limited roles for women) derived from a quest for order among evangelicals late in the nineteenth century. See her *Fundamentalism and Gender: 1875 to the Present* (New Haven, Conn.: Yale University Press, 1993), chap. 2.

47. Despite Title IX provisions, women's athletics still lags behind men's, and in the realm of professional sports women are virtually nonexistent, aside from golf and tennis and now a fledgling basketball league. Even though the San Diego Clippers drafted Iowa basketball whiz Denise Long some years ago, and every so often you read of a female referee or umpire aspiring to make it into the major leagues, women have not been able, for the most part, to break into the male preserve of professional team sports.

48. The only thing that can disrupt this orderly universe is a misjudgment. Nothing enrages a sports dévotée more than a bad call from an official, whose job is to act as an impartial judge and a benign authority figure. The official has no prerogative to be a judicial activist. He cannot hear mitigating arguments before rendering his judgment. A batter thrown out by a step at first base, for example, cannot argue that he should be called safe because had he not injured his ankle back in spring training, he would almost certainly have beaten the throw from shortstop and that to call him out on that play betrayed the umpire's bias against players who are in some way disabled. The wide receiver who failed to plant both feet in bounds before falling out of the end zone cannot argue that he simply forgot to do so and that such negligence should not be held against him and that, furthermore, any adverse ruling would unfairly punish the entire team for the inadvertent lapse of one of its players. No, the officials must render simple, impartial judgments lest they violate the orderly universe that is the world of sports.

49. In every major team sport, the ball represents the world; when the ball stops, play itself stops. In football, which is essentially a military game concerned with the capture and defense of territory, the movement of the ball signals the beginning of play. Basketball, an urban game invented by a YMCA secretary in Springfield, Massachusetts, mimics the urban landscape in that it demands that players maneuver within very narrow confines, similar to those of the urban world itself. Baseball, the only game in which the defense controls the ball, is a game developed and played by immigrants, and it perfectly mirrored their own world. In baseball, the batter is outnumbered nine to one in his attempt to disrupt the defense's control of the game. The defense is malevolently efficient most of the time, and any batter who is successful three times out of ten will probably find a place someday in the Hall of Fame. For the batter, as for the immigrant, the greatest—and most elusive—triumph is to return home, but it is a journey fraught with perils and offering very few islands of safety along the way.

50. Quoted in Ron Fimrite, "Once Powerful, Still Proud," *Sports Illustrated*, 14 October 1996, 8.

51. John M. Murrin, "Rites of Domination: Princeton, the Big Three, and

the Rise of Intercollegiate Athletics," paper delivered at Princeton University, 10 October 1996.

52. Gary Smalley, "Five Secrets of a Happy Marriage," in *Seven Promises of a Promise Keeper* (Colorado Springs: Focus on the Family, 1994), 105.

53. Tony Evans, "Spiritual Purity," in *Seven Promises*, 73, 79.

54. See, for example, James Davison Hunter, *Culture Wars: The Struggle to Define America* (New York: Basic Books, 1991).

55. I've always suspected that the reason for evangelicals' virulent reaction to feminism is that many early leaders of the twentieth-century women's movement were Jewish, which meant that they drew their language, images, and inspiration from sources other than the New Testament and the ideology of nineteenth-century evangelicalism.

Chapter Six: WINNING THE COUNTRY BACK

1. Interview with Duane Gish, in *"In the Beginning": The Creationist Controversy, with Randall Balmer,* 2-part series produced by WTTW-Television, 1994.

2. Ibid.

3. John R. Rice, *Bobbed Hair, Bossy Wives, and Women Preachers* (Murfreesboro, Tenn.: 1941), 15.

4. Ibid., 8.

5. "Address by Patrick J. Buchanan," in *Official Report of the Proceedings of the Thirty-fifth Republican National Convention Held in Houston, Texas, August 17, 18, 19, 20, 1992* (Republican National Committee), 373.

6. "Address by the Reverend Pat Robertson, Virginia Beach, Virginia," ibid., 501, 502.

7. Quoted in Katherine Bishop, "Benicia Journal: Bible and Constitution Clash in a Liberal Land," *New York Times*, 27 August 1990.

8. Quoted in Nicholas Dawidoff, "No Sex. No Drugs. But Rock 'n' Roll (Kind of)," *New York Times Magazine*, 5 February 1995, 44.

9. Quoted in Rob Boston, "Thy Kingdom Come: Christian Reconstructionists Want to Take Dominion over America," *Church & State*, September 1988, 8.

10. Jerry Falwell, *Listen, America!* (Garden City, N.Y.: Doubleday, 1980).

11. Ibid.

12. Thomas B. Edsall, "Forecasting Havoc for Orlando," *Washington Post*, 10 June 1998, A-11; "Pat Robertson Can Be Extreme," *Omaha World-Herald*, 12 June 1998, 22.

13. James Davison Hunter, *Culture Wars: The Struggle to Define America* (New York: Basic Books, 1991).

Index

Church and state, separation of, 4, 31–43, 99–100. *See also* Disestablishment

Church of England, 4, 5, 6, 14, 18, 32, 41, 63

Church of Jesus Christ of Latter-day Saints, 11

Circuit riders, 57, 68

Civil rights movement, 38, 95

Civil War, 58, 59

Clinton, Bill, 95, 106

Clinton, Hillary Rodham, 88, 99, 106, 109

College of New Jersey (Princeton University), 29, 75

Colporteur, 65–67

Columbus, Christopher, 46

Common Sense Realism, 34

Communism, 82, 88–95, 96, 98

Concerned Women for America, 83, 88, 90, 95, 103

Congregationalism, 5, 32, 36

Constitution, 4, 31, 34, 35, 42, 83

Croswell, Andrew, 61–62

Cult of domesticity, 10, 77

Cult of true womanhood, 77, 97, 99

Culture wars, 98, 105–6, 108

Dallas Theological Seminary, 73

Darby, John Nelson, 51

Darwin, Charles, 50, 101

Darwinism, 80

Davenport, James, 61, 62–63

Davies, Samuel, 57

Deists, 4, 63, 100

De Tocqueville, Alexis, 1, 31, 38, 40, 57, 76

Disciples of Christ, 6, 64

Disestablishment, 3–4, 5, 34, 43, 63.

See also Church and state, separation of

Dispensationalism, 51, 55. *See also* Premillennialism

Dobson, James, 81, 95, 104, 109

Dorsius, Peter Henry, 16, 17, 19, 21

Douglas, Ann, 76

Dow, Lorenso, 56, 64

Dowie, John Alexander, 51

Dualism, 59, 92, 96, 98, 99, 106, 107

Duquesne Weekend, 115

Eddy, Mary Baker, 1, 5

Edwards, Jonathan, 11, 18, 47

Eisenhower, Dwight, 39

Enlightenment, 4, 6, 33, 43, 48, 63, 100

Equal Rights Amendment, 82, 83

Evangelical Covenant Church, 27

Evangelical Free Church, 27

Evans, Tony, 90–91

Evolution, 95

Falwell, Jerry, 68, 82, 94, 100, 103, 107, 112

Feminism, 10, 71, 81, 87, 88, 92, 97, 98, 99, 104. *See also* Women's movement

Finney, Charles Grandison, 28, 75, 113

First Amendment, 3, 4, 5, 31, 33, 35, 37, 42, 63

Focus on the Family, 88, 95

Frank, Douglas, 67

Franklin, Benjamin, 62

Freeman, Bernardus, 16, 17, 22–23

Free market of religion, 5, 37, 38, 42, 43, 100, 101

Frelinghuysen, Theodore, 25, 26

Madison, James, 35
Mahan, Asa, 113
Malcolm X, 5
Marsden, George M., 112
Marx, Karl, 35
Mather, Cotton, 74
McCartney, Bill, 84–85, 87, 89, 91, 92
McGuffey Reader, 38
McIntire, Carl, 28, 29
McPherson, Aimee Semple, 28, 57, 67–68
Mead, Sidney E., 31–32
Men and Religion Forward Movement, 86
Merritt, Timothy, 113
Miller, William, 5, 44–46, 49
Moody, Dwight Lyman, 28, 51, 57
Moral Majority, 83, 103
Moravians, 3, 19, 21, 27
Morgan, Marabel, 80, 97
Mormonism, 3, 6, 8, 38, 49–50, 64
Mühlenberg, Heinrich Melchior, 16, 17, 18, 19, 20
Muscular Christianity, 84, 85

Nietzsche, Friedrich, 35
North, Gary, 100
Noyes, John Humphrey, 48

O'Connor, John (Cardinal), 55
Oneida Community, 48
Operation Rescue, 82, 94
Osborne, John Wesley, 65, 66
Ozman, Agnes, 114

Palmer, Phoebe, 75, 113
Parkhurst, Charles H., 59
Pentecostalism, 111, 114, 115
Perot, Ross, 37, 88

Pettingill, William, 51–52
Pickering, Theophilus, 63
Pietism, 6, 9, 14, 15–30, 61
Pilgrims, 74
Pluralism, 3, 4, 102, 103, 106, 108
Pomeroy, Benjamin, 61
Populism, 5, 6–7, 11, 42, 59, 69
Postmillennialism, 1, 47, 48–49, 50, 51
Premillennialism, 47, 51–52, 54, 55. *See also* Dispensationalism
Price, Frederick, 7, 68
Promise Keepers, 71, 84–93
Prosperity theology, 7, 60
Protestant Reformation, 13–14, 32, 56, 65
Puritanism, 2, 6, 7, 8, 9, 11, 14–15, 16, 17, 29, 30, 47, 61, 74

Queen's College (Rutgers University), 19, 28

Ramsey, Andre, 55–56, 69
Reagan, Ronald, 10, 47, 57, 60, 95, 102, 106, 107, 109
Reed, Ralph, 86, 104, 109
Religious Right, 82, 98, 99–100, 101, 102, 104, 106, 107, 108–9
Rice, John R., 79, 97
Robertson, Pat, 10, 94, 98, 100, 104, 107, 109
Robinson, John, 74
Roe v. Wade, 82
Rogers, Nathaniel, 63
Roosevelt, Franklin, 10, 57
Rush, Benjamin, 76, 77
Rushdoony, Rousas John, 100
Russell, Charles Taze, 44

Salem witch trials, 74
Schaff, Philip, 1, 31, 40, 60

Acknowledgments

My intellectual debts are incalculable – and not easily reckoned. The dedication of this book suggests some of what I owe to those who have shaped my thinking about religion in America. Others have contributed as well with criticism, encouragement, and friendship: Nathan O. Hatch, Jan Shipps, Grant Wacker, John R. Fitzmier, Sam Alvord, Harry S. Stout, Judith Weisenfeld, the late G. A. Rawlyk, and many others. I'm grateful for the many audiences over the years, from church forums to Chautauqua, who have listened intently, criticized unstintingly, and asked penetrating questions, thereby helping me to sharpen my arguments. Micah Kleit of Beacon Press gave this manuscript the benefit of his careful scrutiny, as did Chris Kochansky, who is a superb copy editor; any infelicities that remain are mine alone.

My family sustains me in ways that I cannot begin to enumerate. Christian, Andrew, and Sara are the light and delight of my life. My wife, Catharine Randall (yes, her surname is the same as my first name), is my best friend and companion and, to say the least, my most formidable interlocutor. She even puts up with my occasional protestations that I am, after all, a colonial historian.